TREE HOUSES
WITHIN REACH

TREE HOUSES

WITHIN REACH

30 LOFTY CABINS, PLAYHOUSES, AND GETAWAYS
YOU CAN ACTUALLY BUILD

Derek "Deek" Diedricksen

Storey Publishing

The mission of Storey Publishing is to serve our customers by publishing practical information that encourages personal independence in harmony with the environment.

EDITED BY Hannah H. Fries and Sarah Guare Slattery
ART DIRECTION AND COVER DESIGN BY Carolyn Eckert
BOOK DESIGN BY HK Goldstein
TEXT PRODUCTION BY Jennifer Jepson Smith

COVER PHOTOGRAPHY BY © **Chris Daniele/** dirtandglass.net, front l., back t.r.; © **HeshPhoto, Inc.,** front b.r., back b.r., author; **Josh Howell Photography**, back t.l.

INTERIOR PHOTOGRAPHY BY © **Derek Diedricksen**, 3 t., 12, 17–20, 23–25, 28–31, 33–35, 41–46, 48–53, 56–59, 66–71, 93–97, 104–108, 155, 157 l., 159, 163 t., 164, 165, 174, 175, 178, 186, 187 t., 216 t.l.; © **HeshPhoto, Inc.,** IFC, 1, 9, 152, 154, 156, 162, 166, 167, 170, 173, 185, 187 b., 188–215, 216 all but t.l., 217, 224

Jonas Diedricksen, sample tree house construction assistant

Alexandra Diedricksen, sample tree house prop stylist

ADDITIONAL PHOTOGRAPHY CREDITS appear on page 218.

ILLUSTRATIONS BY © **Phil Hackett** (color illustrations); © **Derek Diedricksen** (b & w illustrations); **Alyssa Ly/** © Storey Publishing (arrows, lettering, lines)

TEXT © 2025 by Derek Diedricksen

Take proper safety precautions before using potentially dangerous tools and equipment or undertaking potentially dangerous activities.

The information in this book is true and complete to the best of our knowledge. All recommendations are made without guarantee on the part of the author or Storey Publishing. The author and publisher disclaim any liability in connection with the use of this information.

The publisher is not responsible for websites (or their content) that are not owned by the publisher.

Storey books may be purchased in bulk for business, educational, or promotional use. Special editions or book excerpts can also be created to specification. For details, please contact your local bookseller or the Hachette Book Group Special Markets Department at special.markets@hbgusa.com.

Storey Publishing
210 MASS MoCA Way
North Adams, MA 01247
storey.com

Storey Publishing is an imprint of Workman Publishing, a division of Hachette Book Group, Inc., 1290 Avenue of the Americas, New York, NY 10104. The Storey Publishing name and logo are registered trademarks of Hachette Book Group, Inc.

ISBNs: 978-1-63586-830-2 (paperback); 978-1-63586-831-9 (ebook)

Printed in China by Toppan Leefung Printing Ltd. on paper from responsible sources
10 9 8 7 6 5 4 3 2 1

TLF

Library of Congress Cataloging-in-Publication Data on file

DEDICATION

To my wife, Liz, who has always been beyond supportive of my crazy endeavors, and to my brother Dustin, who has joined me on a good many of them, from Tasmania to Tennessee! Here's to future adventures! And to my parents, Glenn and Sigrid, for allowing that very first tree house.

And an additional shout to those who have helped me on many builds as well—Palo Coleman, Marty Skrelunas, Alex Eaves, and Roy St. Clair. It's been fun trekking around the US with you knuckleheads!

CONTENTS

PART 1: THE TREE HOUSES

SIMPLEST AND MOST AFFORDABLE

MODERATE SKILL AND BUDGET

HIGHLY SKILLED AND BIG BUDGET

PART 2: NUTS AND BOLTS

PART 3: STEP-BY-STEP SAMPLE BUILD

WHY WE LOVE TREE HOUSES:
The Allure of the Skies

A TREE HOUSE IS AN ESCAPE TO NATURE, A HAVEN FROM THE ELEMENTS THAT IS MADE WITHIN THE ELEMENTS.

FROM THEIR LONG and functional use as perches aloft providing safety from the reach of wild animals to their use as surveillance points for hunters, bird-watchers, and young children, tree houses have been around for quite some time, and shall continue to be. Part of their appeal is what I call "the allure of the skies": "What do the birds see? What is *their* vantage? I want to experience it!" But beyond that, they're just outright fun in their unconventional and often primitive basis. They stand as a return to the great outdoors, an escape to nature, as a haven from the elements that is made within the elements.

Their affordability, in some cases, additionally makes them attractive. Having built tree houses for as little as $200 (one featured in this very book) and others almost completely free of cost with the use of found and salvaged materials, I can attest to this. After all, what better and more cost-effective way is there to build a stilted structure than to use stilts that are readily available and plentiful—trees. They are almost everywhere, most of them are incredibly strong (we'll get to that), and they're gorgeous.

Indeed, you could go outside right now and simply put a plank or platform in the boughs of an oak and create a quiet place to read, relax, nap, or observe. That affordable accessibility is most certainly one large factor that keeps these structures in our minds. It is for that very reason that I've included several simple tree houses that don't require many carpentry skills or any fancy tools. Forget crushing mortgages or loans and dismiss the idea of needing a giant team of high-priced contractors and carpenters. *You* could go out and build a tree house today. And I hope you do.

Of course, tree houses run the gamut, from the incredibly simple to masterful, architect-designed floating mansions. A portion of the tree houses I've included aren't so affordable, but each has been chosen for a specific reason, and it is my hope that you'll find loads of ideas even from the tree houses that are beyond your budget. With this book, I hope to help inspire you, if not help you on your way.

JUST WHAT CONSTITUTES A TREE HOUSE?

Purists will argue that a true and legitimate tree house should be one that is solely held up by the tree itself. I mostly agree but give a hall pass to any that are built with a combination of being both attached to trees and supported by posts (or "stilts," as I often call them).

We have included quite a few "tree and stilt" houses in this book, as I feel there is still a lot to be learned from these builds even if the purists aren't as approving of them. All of the stilted structures you see could easily be built in post-less modes, too. Some of their builders and owners simply did not have the luxury of suitable trees to make their builds tree-only ones, and I have a feeling that a good deal of you might fall into that same category. So why not also learn from what they did, and how they went about things?

ARE TREE HOUSES LEGAL?

Codes and allowances vary greatly from town to town, so be sure to look into the local zoning and building codes in your area. There is no "one answer for all" to this question, and you'll have to do a little homework of your own.

I highly recommend you do an online search and take a trip to town hall to ask a few key questions. Also, check in with your neighbors and make sure they are fine with it, especially if it's near a property line or will encroach on their view.

I can't stress this last recommendation enough. Sadly, one of the tree houses in this very book illustrates the unfortunate case of a boundary dispute. This formerly gorgeous, frequently rented, and rather expensive tree house is now a pile of dismantled timber sitting under a tarp in a farm field. Be careful, do some legwork, and make sure that this doesn't happen to you.

MY FIRST TREE HOUSE

MY VERY FIRST TREE HOUSE was made from a platform my father, Glenn, constructed for me. It was as simple as they come, a 4-foot by 4-foot "floor" built with four very wide pieces of dimensional lumber (2×12s) held in place by a series of clever ropes (not one nail in the tree!). I can still feel the spring and bounce of the old spruce's low limbs as I'd climb to it.

It didn't have a ladder, it lacked railings, and it didn't even have a rudimentary roof—it was just a simple perch 12 or so feet in the air, well nestled within a web of tree limbs. It was the 1980s, and this thing was, well, dangerous as heck, but we thought nothing of that.

While I absolutely loved this little tree house, what I recall even more vividly and fondly is the tree itself: its uniqueness and gnarled bent branches, and the enormous and almost tentlike canopy its long branches created below. It was an elevator to secretly look down on the whole expanse of our neighborhood in Madison, Connecticut.

If I were to climb to the very top of the tree until its main trunk became as narrow as my own wrist, swaying and bending under my weight, I could reach a point where my head would break through the ceiling of spruce needles. There, 50 or so feet up in our own little nirvana, my brother Dustin and I were privy to a vantage that was ours and ours alone.

Head high above the pavement of Hamilton Drive below, as the winds of Long Island Sound blew through our hair, we could literally see for miles—the little arched bridge over Fence Creek where we'd go blue-crabbing, neighbors a street or two away on Lawson Drive busy mowing their lawns—it was all there for us to view. And if we were very lucky, we could catch a glimpse of the ice cream truck on its way to the neighborhood, even before the sound of its jingles were audible. It was a special time because it was a special place. Our place.

Years later, when I was at school in Boston, the tree was removed, having grown too large and crowding our neighbors' property line. I remember my mother telling me the news over the phone, and I almost felt as though I had lost a close relative. Memories of the times we had in that corner of our yard flashed by, and I'll admit, to this day, I've gone back there more than a few times to see if any small remnant of the stump remains.

This loss reminds me that the trees themselves, and not just the structures in them, are the elements that make tree houses not only possible but so precious. As any kid that grew up climbing trees knows, to be cradled in the arms of silent giants is something very special indeed.

> IT WAS THE 1980S, AND THIS THING WAS, WELL, DANGEROUS AS HECK, BUT WE THOUGHT NOTHING OF THAT.

A PLUG FOR SIMPLICITY

Everyone seems to love the McMansion-style tree houses. I get it. They're absolutely amazing. But they are also amazingly expensive. Most of us are never going to have the loot to tackle such lofty builds, nor will we have the land or proper trees to attempt such projects.

You're probably already thinking, "Thanks a lot, Mr. Buzzkill Author Guy!"

Hear me out. While those extreme builds are incredible and I love them myself, I am an even bigger fan of what I call "keeping-it-real tree houses." These are the tree houses that most anyone could build with a little education, a decent enough set of specific tools (we'll talk about that later), and a large dash of patience. To me, these simpler tree houses also have a bit more charm in that they're often unlike the homes you and I might already live in. They're rooted in the realm of fantasy and often wind up being rather whimsical with their "build with what ya got" aesthetic. Mega–tree houses, on the other hand, can occasionally come off looking as if a regular home was left relocated and stranded in a tree after a severe tornado. In some cases, big money seems to push thrifty inventiveness into the backseat.

KEY TO TREE HOUSE MATERIALS BUDGETS

$: Under $1,000

$$: $1,000–$9,999

$$$: $10,000–$20,000

$$$$: $20,000–$100,000

$$$$$: Over $100,000

THESE ARE THE TREE HOUSES THAT MOST ANYONE COULD BUILD.

So I've included as many keeping-it-real beginner tree houses as I could find, plus tree houses that require a bit more skill and money, and then, finally, some high-end tree houses that are rather exceptional but still carry that spirit of inventiveness and whimsy. In other words, I tried to work in a little bit of everything for everyone—no easy task.

PART 1

THE TREE HOUSES

BEGINNERS WILL FIND INSPIRATION in the tree houses in the first section— while simple, these builds offer much inventiveness, aesthetic appeal, and overall charm and individuality.

The mid-level tree houses in the next section are a little more costly and perhaps a bit more complicated to build. Some have more involved rooflines, for example, while others have intricate elements that require more patience and know-how.

And finally, the high-end tree houses in the last section were primarily built by longtime professionals and stand on a different plateau when it comes to the skills (patience and know-how) needed to build them. Don't let their big budgets scare you away, though, as they still offer great ideas and layouts and are just, well, really darn cool.

RENEGADE TREE HOUSE

RENEGADE
TREE HOUSE
continued

I HAD LONG BEEN DREAMING of building a "secret" tree house—something to bring me back to the days of my youth, when my brother Dustin and I would scavenge materials and build where no adults in their right minds would dare to chase us and where they wouldn't hear us. I also wanted to clean up the woods I had chosen, while leaving this microbuild as a random and almost magical place. I wanted neighborhood kids to someday find it—a hidden treasure in the woods, a reward for their daring to explore.

Well, fast-forward to a picture of a 44-year-old man—me—who decided to give it a run. My choice of building materials was constrained by the fact that I would have to carry them down a trail and then through unblazed heavy-growth forest and down several hundred feet of a stream. I found that by framing with 2×2 stock, and by lugging out precut planks a few at a time to construct the base, I was able to slowly and secretly construct a tiny little hideaway nap shack deep in the woods. (Time for the disclaimer: I do not recommend that you do as I do. This was all an experiment.)

At about 7 feet long and 3 feet wide, the structure allowed me to lie down, sit upright inside it, and even pop open its hinged roof to make it a bird-watching perch I could stand fully upright in. The nature out there was pretty darn glorious and even included the repeat sightings of the biggest snapping turtle I've ever seen, and I've seen a lot of them.

LOCATION: Can't tell ya—in fact, you know too much already . . .

SIZE: 21 square feet

BUDGET: $

DESIGNER/BUILDER:
Derek "Deek" Diedricksen

AMENITIES: Lots of fresh air and "nonstop running water"

Here is my secret place for reading, writing, and relaxing.

I WANTED NEIGHBORHOOD KIDS TO SOMEDAY FIND IT— A HIDDEN TREASURE IN THE WOODS, A REWARD FOR THEIR DARING TO EXPLORE.

RENEGADE
TREE HOUSE
continued

Safety Note

Nothing about this build is conventional or even really recommended. This was another reason that I wanted to keep things very small in scale. I don't recommend the post-in-the-water approach (unless we're talking huge, treated dock posts), but I had little other choice as I didn't want to further burden this crooked, Seussian tree with any guy lines or metal cable supports. After all, it had already fallen over once and then rerooted.

Two years later, the post is still straight as an arrow and doing its job. In a year or two, I might tiptoe back out there to replace it. Basically, building in a soft-soil wetlands area, never mind within a body of water, is never a structurally fantastic idea—it comes with its challenges.

Since there is a good chance that a structure like this could be vandalized down the road, I built it from found junk and scraps, not wanting to break the bank on something that wasn't my own. I'll also add that the Sunlite Multiwall polycarbonate panel wall was a time- and weight-saver and gave the interior such a cool—and larger—feel. This stuff is now popular in tree houses, as it is easy to cut, haul, and install, and I feel it gives even the most hokey and rustic tree house a little bit of a modern vibe.

ROBOT
TREE HOUSE

LOCATION: Orleans, Vermont

SIZE: 40 square feet

BUDGET: $

DESIGNER/BUILDER:
Derek "Deek" Diedricksen

AMENITIES: None
(a bare-bones shelter)

ROBOT
TREE HOUSE
continued

FOR LACK OF A BETTER NAME, we dubbed this whimsical edifice the Robot Tree House. As they say, "If the shoe fits . . . ," although in this case I suppose it might be some sort of mechanized, steel-clad, size 42 cyborg shoe.

Built in the summer of 2016 in a hands-on Relaxshacks workshop (a series of hands-on building and design classes based off my blog), the goal of this particular project was not only to give students some basic knowledge in the field of tree house construction but also to find inspiration through the money-saving means of reuse and salvage. Many of the pine boards in this project were pulled from an old house that was to be demolished, while other boards were harvested from the side of the road on various trash days. You'd be surprised at the amount of usable construction materials you are bound to find for absolutely nothing if you keep your eyes peeled.

Safety Note

A simple bit of advice: If you end up building anything tall up on posts, be sure to brace it well to prevent wobbling or racking (coming out of shape or out of plumb). Even short little picnic tables employ triangular bracing to minimize movement and to strengthen the structure as a whole. With this Robot Tree House, we went "full-out fire tower," as I call it, and added front cross-bracing to keep it from shifting while it had occupants. This method works very well and has been employed in bridge building for centuries.

Here's an example of Suntuf roofing being used as a clear exterior wall covering.

ROBOT
TREE HOUSE
continued

While deciding to use only reused items for a build can be limiting, I feel that it also makes a project even more fun. The roof of this structure is a great example of that. Built out of discarded post-election coroplast yard signs (a friend of mine ran for a school committee), the roof was made with zero new materials aside from the roofing screws. The all-weather poly/plastic panels more or less served as giant shingles, and though they do make for a very unattractive roof, with the tree house roof being 23 feet in the air, they aren't seen by anyone from the ground.

Lastly, this is yet another tree house that uses Suntuf clear panels to create a large wall to bring in a ton of natural light. This makes the space feel far larger than it really is, and it creates quite a dramatic lighting effect at night: The "thorax" of this huge creature lights up as if it were an enormous lantern. At my Relaxshacks workshops, we do nighttime demos and DIY talks by the light of this build.

Hindsight Is 20/20

Here is a perfect example of where an access hatch does not work. The smaller the square footage of your build, the more usable floor space a hatch ends up eating.

This tree house was built with just enough floor space to barely fit two sleeping bags or a full-size air mattress; beyond that there is very little space to maneuver and even less to get to the hatch once your bedding is set up. It makes for an awkward space if you plan on sleeping in it. Just something to consider.

I will add that the hatch is unintentionally located in a somewhat comical spot, especially as you watch people descend down the ladder from it, so be sure to keep everyday use in mind when deciding where to place your hatch.

YOU'D BE SURPRISED AT THE AMOUNT OF USABLE CONSTRUCTION MATERIALS YOU ARE BOUND TO FIND FOR ABSOLUTELY NOTHING IF YOU KEEP YOUR EYES PEELED.

MAGIC BULLET
TREE HOUSE

WHY SPEND MONEY OR BE SO QUICK TO TOSS SOMETHING OUT WHEN SOME OF THE VERY "WASTE" AT HAND STILL HAS LIFE IN IT?

WHAT CAN I SAY? This truck bed and cap held aloft on a tree stump is hokey, goofy, simple, and even a bit comical . . . and that is why I love it. Builds that are unique and use repurposed materials always nab my attention. While this one is incredibly bare-bones, it drives home the idea that even unexpected things can be used as the basis of a tree house. Giant wooden shipping crates, old car shells, ice-fishing tents—they all could work on a perched platform. While they'd never end up in an issue of *Better Homes & Gardens*, why not consider them if you don't have much money for a build?

Truck bed caps are tossed very frequently, as are old truck bodies and trucks themselves, making them easy to salvage. This build also keeps more material from the landfill, from the upcycled playmats as cushioning to the ramshackle piece of metal roofing as an overhang. Why spend money or be so quick to toss something out when some of the very "waste" at hand still has life in it?

Most people will criticize any structure in which one can't fully stand up, but when you're creating small sleeping pods/units and working with a very limited budget, the extra height often isn't necessary. There is also a certain childlike charm in crawl structures, perhaps evoking memories of building blanket forts as a kid.

I also love how these folks have let the landscape and foliage envelop and almost overtake the structure, so that it looks as if it belongs there. The natural railings and the repurposed-tire steps all help to set the stage for the inventive fun of this little sleep chamber.

And while some might scoff at boxy structures, keep in mind that there is something to be said for basic and vernacular design: It works, it's cheap to construct, and it doesn't require an abacus to figure out each cut. The only worry with building anything so cubelike is rain runoff, but that is something that could be remedied easily. And runoff is not a concern in this case, as truck bed caps are designed to be waterproof and are contoured for drainage.

This tree house has been rented out to countless campers—clear and present proof that even adults are more than fine with a low-ceiling, fortlike, repurposed-materials rental. And the campground on which it is located, loaded with funky little pods and glamping stations for rent, is a lo-fi, no-frills retreat of sorts.

LOCATION: Baying Hound Campground, Asheville, North Carolina

SIZE: 34 square feet (standard size of a truck bed)

BUDGET: $

DESIGNERS: Bobby McMasters (setting), Ben Jundanian (exterior art), Michaella Sheridan (interior art)

AMENITIES: Solar lights

FOR THE
BIRDS

THIS SIMPLE AND AFFORDABLE tree house could be built in a weekend. Its huge triangular floor was built in halves so as to enable easy transport down an incredibly steep hill. These were placed on two girders that were installed on site.

If you look closely, you'll see that every pound of this structure is held aloft by two trees; there isn't a single pole aiding the structure. The majority of support for this build comes from the diagonal bracing with 2×8s from underneath, and the girder cradles on the tree carry the rest of the weight.

LOCATION: Augusta, Maine

SIZE: 32 square feet

BUDGET: $

DESIGNER/BUILDER: Derek "Deek" Diedricksen

AMENITIES: None (a bare-bones observation shelter)

Because it is a tree house at a summer-only residence, we didn't want access to it to be too easy or enticing (to avoid kids getting hurt and vandalism), so a portable ladder is brought to the little hut in season.

This is one of the few tree houses in this collection that is not totally enclosed. Built roughly 10 feet off the ground, the shelter affords a view above the tall grass of the marsh onto a very private cove with an abundance of wildlife. As it turns out, this spot happens to be the fishing grounds of a great blue heron, which we've observed feeding several times. By being above the bird's line of sight—not to mention those of other creatures—this little build is great for quiet observation. The view was so spectacular that I didn't even want glass or Plexiglas getting in the way, never mind 2×4 framing to support and affix such items. The result is something somewhat resembling a small scout camp lean-to, but aloft.

Safety Notes

Since buying TAB (tree house attachment bolts) hardware would have immediately doubled my almost nonexistent budget, I used lag screws (large, heavy-duty screws with hex heads) on this one. They have been in place for years without problems, though I do have to back them out a half-turn or so every year as the tree widens when it grows. Modern hardware is the way to go, but this old method still works with smaller builds and the right setup (with the caveat of needing some attention and maintenance in the years down the road).

Always avoid building too close to the water because of the issue of soil saturation (tree roots are less stable). This tree house was a good 10 feet or more away from the water's edge and quite a ways uphill.

A drop-down screen to protect against insects may be a good idea for an open build like this, though mosquitoes don't really seem to enter this space. (Fun fact: Mosquitoes generally don't fly at heights greater than 25 feet—one argument, perhaps, for building very high up in a tree.)

Finally, I left as many branches as possible, as I do often with my tree house builds, so that the structure feels naturally enveloped or "hugged" by the trees. The pine boughs that drape in front of the build provide shade for the house's inhabitants and make them virtually invisible to the birds, as well as to the occasional motorboat or kayak that passes through the area.

THE SNAIL

AMONG THE SMALLEST of the tree houses in this book, it relies solely on the trees for support. The Snail was a microbudget build at one of our hands-on Tiny House Summer Camp workshops in northern Vermont. It served as a design exercise in "thinking-outside-the-box construction."

This little guy is so tiny that it really only sleeps one average-to-large adult—and only if that adult sleeps diagonally. It will fit two sleepers that are shorter in stature (say, 5 foot 8 and under). This size was intentional, as we were experimenting with constructing mini homeless shelters that could be built for almost nothing with the intention of keeping people out of the elements, even just temporarily. It was also an example of "build with what ya got," and we just didn't have many longer boards. By being so very tiny, it is also easy to hide or camouflage.

LOCATION: Vermont's Northeast Kingdom (on the grounds of Relaxshacks Tiny House Summer Camp)

SIZE: 38 square feet

BUDGET: $

DESIGNER/BUILDER: Derek "Deek" Diedricksen and friends/workshop students

AMENITIES: Nonc/off grid

THE
SNAIL
continued

Safety Notes

I've used this tree house as a sort of an experiment and would not recommend this approach. It is held up by lag screws, and while I'd normally back them out a half-turn or so every year to allow for tree growth and movement, I have chosen not to, keeping tabs on what happens. The tree is slowly engulfing the board and growing around it, so that the board is now almost inset on a bulged ledge of the tree as the widening trunk has expanded beneath it. If anything, this seems to give the supports additional bolstering. It is doing so on one small area of each supportive tree, so I don't feel it will do much damage to the trees over time.

The TimberLOK screws (heavy-duty wood screws) have not given way or snapped, nor have their flange heads been sucked into the board. I'm also keeping an eye on the bark near the junction to make sure I'm not promoting trapped water or rot, but so far all is good.

Laying wood batten strips near the outward edges of the tar-paper roof is also a great idea to keep the ends from coming loose in high winds, which would ultimately lead to the roof's demise.

This aerial pod was cobbled together from free scraps and salvaged and roadside materials, though we did use new Suntuf panels and a few pressure-treated 2×8s. It was intentionally designed to be very lightweight, since it was built in panels that had to be carried a quarter of a mile into the woods across very uneven terrain. A good deal of the framing was made with 2×2s and it was clad in low-density Northern White Cedar. Because of this, the whole tree house was so light that when preassembled and tested, it could be lifted off the ground by just two people. This "daintiness" enabled its thinner cradle members and diagonal bracing to suffice, and it has sat in the same spot, unaltered and untroubled, for almost nine years now.

The ladder, too, was built from lumber we already had on hand. The angular cuts to each step end were made for aesthetics and to give the tree house and its ladder an almost UFO look. Many say that "the UFO" would have been a better name for this one.

The tar-paper roof was an unintended experiment, as we were running out of time during our weekend-long workshop and couldn't install anything more traditional. It held up surprisingly well for over six years, so when it was time for a replacement, we just stapled another fresh layer or two of tar paper over it, allowing for some overhang. A roof like this is ugly, yes, but it's so high up that only the birds will really see it.

IT SERVED AS A DESIGN EXERCISE IN "THINKING-OUTSIDE-THE-BOX CONSTRUCTION."

THE ISOLATION POD

CALLED "A PLACE OF HEALING" by its owner/builder, Carsten Ginsburg, this little glass-enclosed tree house lies in the woods of British Columbia. It's another tree house that is elevated by its dreamscape-like locale.

A solar-powered USB lighting system illuminates both the interior and exterior of this little cabin in the trees with minimal difficulty and even less by way of expense. At night, exterior lights allow Ginsburg to observe the curious creatures of the woods that pass by and check out his humble part-time abode. Occasionally even a grizzly bear or two will walk by to see what all the woodland commotion is about. It's a reverse aquarium of sorts where the occupant can stay high, dry, and safe, while observing the natural state of the flora and passing fauna.

LOCATION: Central Coast, British Columbia

SIZE: 75 square feet

BUDGET: $

DESIGNER/BUILDER: Carsten Ginsburg

AMENITIES: Solar USB lighting and diesel heater

The abundance of windows (all cut from salvaged plate glass to save money) help prevent this interior space from feeling too claustrophobic. "It's a place to immerse myself in nature, so I wanted it to have an open feel. I love being there in the winter when it's snowing—it's extra beautiful," explains Ginsburg. And while a space with this much glass might tend to get too cold in the winter months in Canada, a diesel heater, located on an outside platform (for proper ventilation), remedies that.

Inside, the layout is based on the arrangement of Ginsburg's sailboat—compact and efficient. A space-saving chair transforms into a bed, and a small gas-powered burner sits on a shelf.

With little prior building experience, Ginsburg first assembled the wall pieces of his tree house in his garage, only to later cart them to their present site for assembly. Access to tools and the ability to do a good deal of his construction at home allowed him the luxury of both time and convenience.

FAVORITE FEATURE

This is one of my favorite tree houses in the book, as it's so unassuming yet so effective. By cantilevering the glass walls outward in his design, Ginsburg provides a better view of the forest floor below and avoids making this tree house a mere glass box. You soon realize that the seeming sparseness of this tree house's interior is offset by the busyness of the forest backdrop. There is no lack of things to look at—no wall art needed.

And while it may lack privacy—as some will be quick to point out—it's also located so deep in the woods that this need not be a concern. Besides, curtains would be incredibly easy to install if you did need to go that route.

"IT'S A PLACE TO IMMERSE MYSELF IN NATURE."

FOR THE KIDS . . .
LOTS OF KIDS

MADE FOR A CLIENT, this tree house is a good example of a generally affordable build. This one was intended for kids—my client's seven children, all of whom needed a play or hangout space. Versatility became the key here, as the kids ranged in age from elementary to high school. Ultimately, I opted for lots of natural light and vibrant color.

By keeping the design as open and undivided as possible, you can make the smallest of spaces seem just a hair bigger than they are. The mini lofted bed area created some additional hangout space in the upper region of this box-like build, but it also broke the monotony of it being a boring cube within. Add a built-in seat platform, which creates the opportunity for hidden storage beneath, and you start to maximize what little you have.

Don't forget about what's outside the tree house. I particularly like the multi-level deck and walkway. Kids just seem to love having multiple perches and platforms to sit, climb, and play on. I call this the "Ewok Village" look. It gives any tree house a grander appearance. It's easier to do with tree houses that stand at a lower height, another reason why I try not to build too high when kids are involved (aside from the obvious safety concerns). As author and humorist Douglas Adams said, "It's not the fall that kills you; it's the sudden stop at the end."

LOCATION: Stoughton, Massachusetts

SIZE: 56 square feet

BUDGET: $$

DESIGNER/BUILDER: Derek "Deek" Diedricksen

AMENITIES: Electricity by extension cord

Finally, kids love color. You'll seldom find a kid who goes out of their way to ask for their bedroom to be painted a bland white or gunmetal gray. So I went for bold color on the interior. Adult tree houses are a different story, and going with a natural look in that case certainly makes sense. Just something to keep in mind.

Safety Notes

I used 6×6 pressure-treated posts to build this one, as small as it is. Sure, I could have used 4×4s, but the larger boards lent more strength. The last thing I wanted was seven kids and their seven friends plummeting to the ground while horsing around in this structure. I built it to a standard I often refer to as "elephant-proof," to ensure it would be enjoyed for years and years.

And while this was considered a solo build, I did enlist help to carry the wall panels from my trailer to the site, and then to hoist them 7 feet or so into the air. Even if you're framing with mere 2×2 or 2×3 stock, these walls get heavy real fast and are even more perilous to move in high winds. In fact, don't ever try lifting walls of any tree house into place when it's windy out. You're bound to get hurt—really, really hurt. I believe that level of hurt can aptly be described by the term *dead*.

A-FRAME

TREE HOUSE

YOU DON'T OFTEN SEE A-frame tree houses, which surprises me, as they are so incredibly easy to build; I mean, the walls and the roof are the very same. Perhaps the fact that their slanted walls lead to a lot of head bumping is the culprit, as many seem to find them awkward and spatially inefficient. Still, I do feel that their ease of construction often outweighs this shortcoming.

Faced with limited time and travel, I decided to use the A-frame approach for this tree house for my friend's kid, Orion. To minimize the claustrophobic feeling of a steeply descending roof, I added 30-inch knee walls on either side. This also adds headroom as well as more usable dry space beneath the canopy.

LOCATION: Madison, Connecticut

SIZE: 52 square feet

BUDGET: $$

DESIGNER/BUILDER: Derek "Deek" Diedricksen

AMENITIES: None

SAFETY NOTES

ADD PADDING UNDER ZIP LINES.
Everybody loves zip lines, but they're kind of dangerous, especially when the takeoff point is 8 feet in the air. If you ever do go for this high-launch approach, I would suggest adding a rather large pile of mulch right beneath the takeoff edge. This way if anyone were to let go or accidentally step off the edge, they're not landing on hard ground, roots, a stone wall, or anything that would result in serious injury. It's a little extra step and expense that is more than worth it.

OVERESTIMATE ZIP LINE WEIGHT.
Furthermore, be sure to buy a zip line whose rated load capacity far exceeds the weights of the passengers that you expect will be using it. I was the very first to try this installation out. Clocking in around 230 pounds, I figured that if I were held up, the zip line would hold most anyone.

BUILD SCAFFOLDING.
I want to add that A-frame roofs can be very dangerous to install on a tree house because of their steep slope. With Orion's tree house, I made sure to erect a scaffolding setup so that I could more easily access the roof while attaching the Suntuf. Sure, the scaffolding took an hour or so to set up, but it beat breaking my back in a fall.

Tree house work can be very dangerous, so be cautious and don't be tempted by careless shortcuts. Many builders even wear tree-climbing harnesses for their aerial work, which is never a bad idea—especially for extraordinarily high builds.

A-FRAME
TREE HOUSE
continued

MY MINDSET WITH BUILDS IS TO ALWAYS BE FLUID AND OPEN TO CHANGE OR EVEN IMPROVISATION WHEN THE SPARK OR OPPORTUNITY ARISES.

I also made the front wall out of Sunlite Multiwall polycarbonate, so that the space is bright and feels less enclosed. On top of that, the A-shape window can drop open, thus enabling the entire tree house interior to be open to nature when needed. A small, thin door also prevented me from eating up too much of the limited wall space if shelving, art, and hung decorations were to be added later on. Finally, a simple little deck and a lengthy zip line provide more outdoor enjoyment.

My mindset with builds is to always be fluid and open to change or even improvisation when the spark or opportunity arises. So when I saw that the natural crotch of the tree stood out as an obvious place to install a small sitting bench, I constructed a perch from materials that were left over from the build. This created a perfect little reading spot, and, while entirely unplanned, it added more fun and appeal to the build overall.

CORKE FAMILY
TREE HOUSE

I LOVE BUILDING TREE HOUSES FOR FAMILIES, even when the budgets are meager, as I know I'm helping parents create memories for their kids—memories that might last a lifetime. This tree house, based off a small lean-to–like cabin I had designed years prior, was built with a fairly small budget for the three daughters in the Corke family.

I built an ample-size deck first, which gave me more than enough room to carry, maneuver, and place the preassembled pieces onto the platform. This deck also provided a clean place to arrange materials, make cuts, and cleanly store tools. I recommend this approach if time, money, and space allow. Tree houses that have a larger deck or landing are just easier and less risky to work on once that deck is up and running.

LOCATION: Massachusetts

SIZE: 48 square feet

BUDGET: $$

DESIGNER/BUILDER:
Derek "Deek" Diedricksen

AMENITIES: None/off grid

Though simple and cost-effective, this tree house looks more modern and high-end with a few simple material choices and accents. The deck adds usable space, and the large clear front wall made of Suntuf makes the tree house seem larger on the inside. We were sure to retain some play area beneath the tree house, too, a 7-foot-high space that could potentially provide room to hang a future swing or hammock.

At around 6 feet deep and 8 feet long, this tree house is large enough for two average-size adults to sleep and stretch out, should the family ever want to offer up the space to guests. Just blow up an air mattress, and you're good to go!

The steep slant of the roof means that while you can stand at the high end as you enter, the back end of the tree house requires some more intimate crouching. I personally like this approach or look in tree houses, but it can be a "head slammer" for adults. Another option would be to install some Suntuf panels as skylights, especially if you were in a shaded forest and wanted even more natural light.

CORKE FAMILY
TREE HOUSE
continued

FAVORITE FEATURE

Not to sound like a broken record, but the usable deck space is what I like the most. While not all that large, it still adds quite a bit of additional living and play space. For an adult, it would be a great little spot to set up a pair of chairs and a tiny cocktail table for evening drinks or a meal. I could have added more standing space by making this build boxier, too, but that would have significantly changed the look of everything.

HOBBIT HOUSE

DESIGNED BY DAVID AND JEANIE STILES, the author/architect duo of countless books in the design field, the Hobbit House is a sequel of sorts to an earlier Hobbit-influenced tree house they had built. It forgoes the usual underground or hill-embedded approach we're used to seeing with anything Tolkien-related, yet it still looks like a place where hobbits would live. The huge circular door is the main focal point that speaks to the hobbit idea and allows the interior to be open to fresh air and sunlight in good weather.

LOCATION: Long Island, New York

SIZE: Approx. 64 square feet

BUDGET: N/A

ARCHITECTURAL DESIGNERS: David and Jeanie Stiles, Stiles Designs

AMENITIES: Electrical outlets

This portal door is a great example of going all-out with one specific element that is bound to turn heads. Circular doors are a bit challenging to frame and hang with proper support—especially with their cantilevered weight—but they sure make a big impact. And if you're a Tolkien fan and want to make quite a visual statement at first glance, then it's certainly something to consider, as these round doors are the key visual element of hobbit homes.

This is another great (and fun) example of just how much color you can add to a space. It also shows that you *can* have a tree house–like vibe even if the necessary trees are not available. I especially love the whimsical look of both the interior (note the little fake potbellied woodstove) and the exterior, with its little railing and trim details. The Stileses are certainly a duo to look into, as they've been immersed in the DIY-building and "cool cabins" game as authors and designers/builders for decades. I highly recommend their book *Cabins: A Guide to Building Your Own Nature Retreat* to folks looking for budget-build concepts, and their book *Rustic Retreats* also has some great ideas that are easy to execute.

A LOFTED ART STUDIO

ONCE ADULTS DISCOVER HOW FUN and cozy tree houses are, they tend to move in—and sometimes even take over. With that in mind, I designed this tree house to be both kid-cool and adult-feasible.

I aimed for an open and airy space, thereby making the most of such a tiny footprint. If I added dividers or built-ins, this small interior would have felt many times smaller than it actually is. It's basically one open room with a salvaged ladder and landing (both incredibly small) and a long, thin desk (a freebie cut from a portion of a roadside table from trash day). And by keeping the space open, the owners would have the freedom of adding whatever they wanted: a small armchair, ottoman, or whatever else.

LOCATION: Boston, Massachusetts, area

SIZE: 54 square feet and another 26 in the loft

BUDGET: $$

DESIGNER/BUILDER: Derek "Deek" Diedricksen

AMENITIES: None

A LOFTED ART STUDIO

continued

As I envisioned both kids and adults wanting to paint and create art in such a space, I lugged in a huge salvaged slider window (7 by 6 feet). I knew from the start that this would be one of the focal points of the room. By using this window, I saved money (again, it was free), I gobbled up wall space that otherwise would be created with expensive wood, and I expanded the view.

I added some additional light and a funky flair to the tree house by scrapping together a bizarre angular front wall with clear Suntuf roofing and a variety of shorter scrap boards I had saved. This wall includes an inset triangular hatch, also made of scrap wood, that opens for additional fresh air. The abundance of light and large windows really makes the space feel larger than it is, connecting it to the outdoors.

Furthermore, the comparatively high ceiling and the small loft also lend a sense of larger space to this studio. I was careful not to eat up all the visual space with the micro loft, so it is open on two ends, allowing kids to peek down from either side when lounging up there. The downside, of course, is that there are two sides of the loft from which little kids might fall (the reason we installed railings).

FAVORITE FEATURE

The enormous slider window really makes this space by creating a massive view of the forest beyond. It's almost as if this tree house is a woodland fish tank.

Finally, I was able to achieve what I call "cheated height" by choosing a set of trees (maples) that were on the side of a hill. The higher side of the tree house, which has the main viewing window, is about 11 feet in the air, while the lower side with the entrance is about 5 feet high. Because of this, I only had to lift materials up about 5 feet but was able to build higher with ease.

WINE, DINE, AND
UNWIND

WHEN BUILDER/DESIGNER MICHAEL SCAGLIONE was approached by interior designer Kristen Yonson of SwatchPop! to help craft an ideal backyard entertainment spot for adults, this rather classy stilt house was born. While no suitable trees were available—the plight of a great many tree houses—Scaglione and crew quickly drafted up a stilted concept that would still give the desired sense of tree house height, but with the stability and safety of a platform deck. The end result is this gorgeous three-season space.

Here the owners can host dinner parties and later lounge with cocktails by the campfire ring below the tree house. Or take a swing. This tree house was also situated so that a pull-down movie screen could be hung opposite it, thus enabling people in the tree house as well as those lounging below it to watch drive-in–style movies at night.

LOCATION: Milton, Georgia

SIZE: 196-square-foot deck with a 96-square-foot house

BUDGET: $$

DESIGNER/BUILDER: Firefly Forts

AMENITIES: Electricity

The great French doors make a huge deal of sense. One could open them up when they wanted a natural breeze and to feel closer to the elements. Conversely, in colder months, these doors, when left closed, would still allow in a wealth of natural sunlight (solar gain, a.k.a. "free heat").

To save money and achieve a more bespoke or rustic look, you could use salvaged or found second-hand French doors. It pays to look around a bit before laying hammer to nails. You might not only discover a means to saving money but also find elements and materials that far exceed your initial expectations.

This tree house is another example of how you don't need a Vanderbilt Mansion–size budget to make a place where everyone wants to hang out. With some strategic lighting, a rug, and a table with a nice tablecloth, this simple tree house was elevated into an incredibly attractive entertaining space. It's certainly a setting I'd love to be invited to for a dinner party. I think they call this "outdoing the Joneses," but all within a fairly modest budget.

WINE, DINE, AND UNWIND

continued

"YOU DON'T NEED A VANDERBILT MANSION-SIZE BUDGET TO MAKE A PLACE WHERE EVERYONE WANTS TO HANG OUT."

Like most of the other
builds I've done using
Sunlite Multiwall panels,
this tree house takes on a
whole other look when lit
up at night.

BUMBLEBUG
TREE HOUSE

WHILE NOT THE ONLY robot-themed tree house that I've built (see the Robot Tree House on page 21), the Bumblebug (owner's name) stands out because its head is an old Volkswagen Beetle trunk lid. It also holds the odd distinction of being the world's very first robot tree house rental—yes, you can spend a night in it, or 10.

LOCATION: New Market, Alabama, at Leigh Acres

SIZE: 50 square feet

BUDGET: $$

DESIGNER/BUILDER: Derek "Deek" Diedricksen

AMENITIES: Electricity via nearby cord/exterior outlet and bathroom nearby

Here's the early phase of the Bumblebug before we started building the interior bunk beds and such.

BUMBLEBUG
TREE HOUSE
continued

This whimsical house was erected as part of a hands-on Relaxshacks building workshop with students over a mere two days. It resides on a funky, artsy, and salvage-themed compound dubbed Leigh Acres after its owner and founder, Leigh Daniel. The property also features a myriad of cool camper conversions, tiny houses, a micro A-frame, farm animals, and quite a bit more—including a stage for a variety of events.

As for the robot, the interior is very small, with just enough room for bunk beds, which is always a decent idea in very small tree houses, though the additional sleep space comes at the expense of a little visual space. The Sunlite Multiwall—covered flip-open front gives an added dose of uniqueness. When you desire a bit of airflow, or a view of the nearby pond, just prop open the awning window.

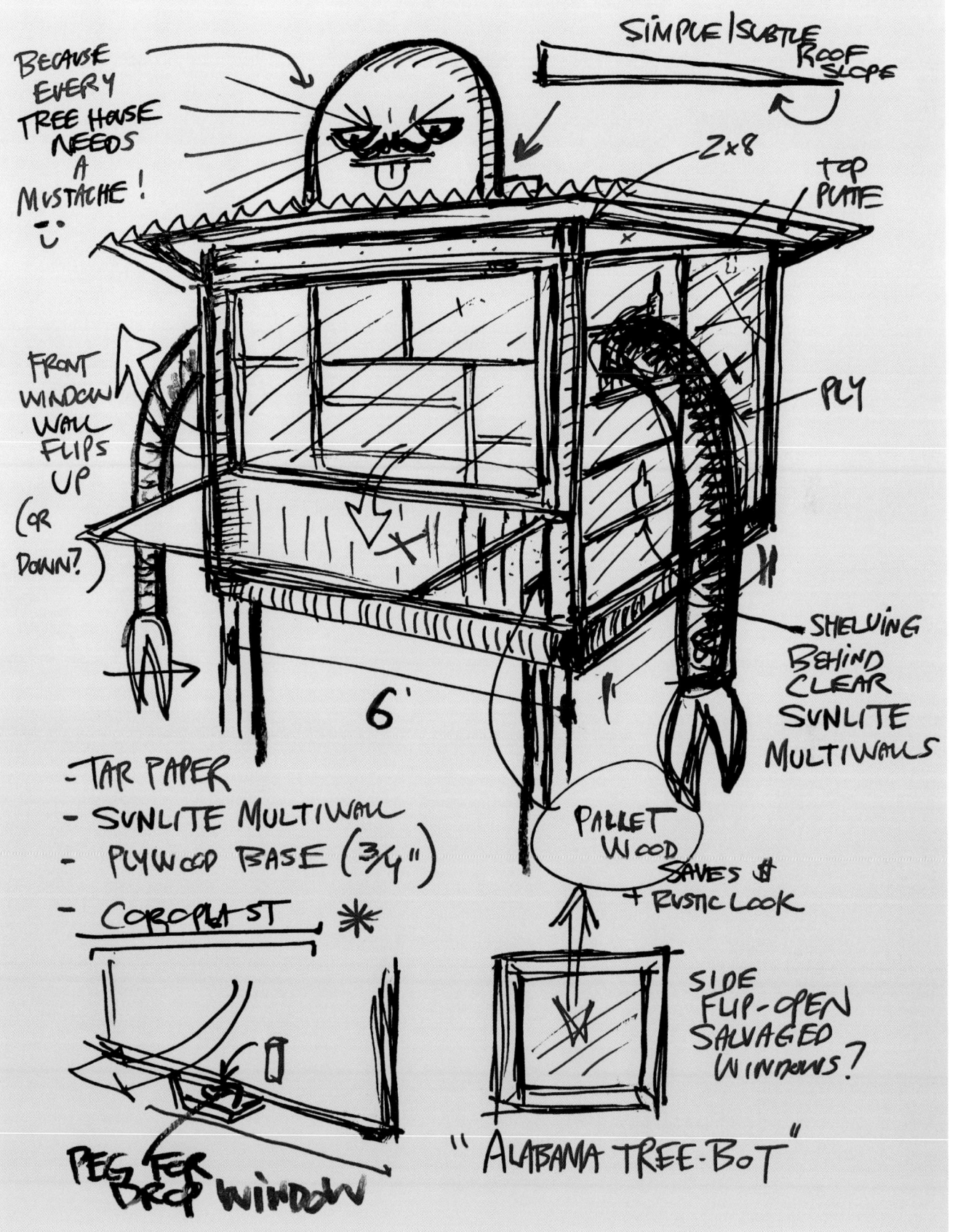

BECAUSE EVERY TREE HOUSE NEEDS A MUSTACHE! ☺

SIMPLE/SUBTLE ROOF SLOPE

2×8

TOP PLATE

PLY

FRONT WINDOW WALL FLIPS UP (OR DOWN?)

6'

SHELVING BEHIND CLEAR SUNLITE MULTIWALLS

- TAR PAPER
- SUNLITE MULTIWALL
- PLYWOOD BASE (3/4")
- COROPLAST ✳

PALLET WOOD SAVES $ + RUSTIC LOOK

SIDE FLIP-OPEN SALVAGED WINDOWS?

PEG FOR DROP WINDOW

"ALABAMA TREE-BOT"

We intentionally made the space beneath the stilt legs of this robot tall enough so most people could stand upright. This makes it a shady space for hanging out or a place to sit out the rain while staying high and dry (or low and dry?). It's also an ideal spot to hang a seat or a swing or set up a built-in bar or dining table. Some have even gone so far as to screen in such spaces, creating a refuge from mosquitoes. Others might install a deck platform. Just be warned that this will drastically change the look of your structure. It will look far less like a tree house and quite a bit more like a giant tower instead.

Safety Note

Be sure that you have ample swing space inside and outside a swinging door. Too little of that, and access becomes a bit dangerous. Many who construct small spaces might opt to have a door swing outward as it saves indoor space, but just be sure to have enough space on the landing to make this safe and possible.

PEREGRINE
PERCH

PEREGRINE PERCH was built as an off-grid retreat for its owner. Located in Dragon Hollow on 30 acres backed up to Pisgah National Forest, it is surrounded by mature hardwoods and abundant wildlife. The goal in building it was to blend this hillside tree house with the natural wooded environment, with minimal damage to that ecosystem.

Although it's basically a "tree" house (Fen, its owner, lived here full-time one summer), the Perch does not use living trees as its structural members. Instead, posts were partially concealed by dead tree trunk lengths cut to shape, and natural elements from the landscape were added, including grapevines and branches, to create the tree house aesthetic. Using on-site materials also enabled builder Chris Strathy (a.k.a. The Capable Carpenter) to keep the build within the very small budget he was handed.

LOCATION: Lenoir, North Carolina

SIZE: 94 square feet

BUDGET: $$

DESIGNERS/BUILDERS: Chris Strathy (a.k.a. The Capable Carpenter) and volunteers

AMENITIES: Woodstove for heat (soon) and composting toilet nearby

FAVORITE FEATURES

The wraparound deck really adds useful living space to this build, especially in a state with a longer stretch of warm weather, such as North Carolina. Not only can you hang out here, but it's also the cooking hub with the outdoor truck-box-turned-kitchen. A good idea, since you wouldn't want to smoke out a mere 94-square-foot tree house were you to include the kitchen and stove inside.

The small sleep loft above saves floor space in the downstairs and allows for privacy when needed. A set of narrow windows gives those in the loft a higher vantage point. Be sure that you don't skimp on windows in a loft such as this, and plan ahead so that your morning view is a scenic one. As I tell people, "Aim for the mountains, not the smokestacks."

The windows, door, vintage kitchen storage unit, trim, and other elements were all repurposed, giving the overall space a rustic and lived-in feel. Some of these second-life items not only saved Fen money but also freed up space, such as the refinished antique tea cart with storage beneath that additionally folds out to become a table. Even the outdoor kitchen was crafted from a repurposed truck box that was turned on its side—a very clever idea.

MICHAEL'S MEMORIAL

THIS TREE HOUSE was built for Michael of Warren, Vermont, when he was dying of pancreatic cancer. Michael wanted to do something special for his kids before passing—something they could remember him by—so he asked builder James "B'fer" Roth to build him a tree house. Roth and many volunteers in the town, including Michael's wife and kids, came together to build this in time for Michael to see and appreciate it.

While only 150 square feet, this tree house manages to pack in a lot of fun touches. The snowshoe embedded in a door that serves as a sort of window is one. Another is a door featuring a bicycle wheel window and a baseball serving as a door handle. While borderline odd to some, the approach is rather daring, serving a purpose while also highlighting the playful and creative spirit of this house and the man it pays tribute to. It also exemplifies the beauty of free experimentation in less costly structures, where you're at liberty to try on some "out there" ideas when less money is on the line.

LOCATION: Warren, Vermont

SIZE: 150 square feet

BUDGET: N/A

DESIGNERS/BUILDERS: B'fer Roth and the loving community of Warren

AMENITIES: None

MICHAEL'S MEMORIAL

continued

The crooked roof is another very noticeable facet, giving this memorial an almost surreal Salvador Dalí look. These crooked and twisted lines broadcast the message "This is supposed to be fun. We're not taking ourselves too seriously here—let's forget the rules for just a bit." And is that not some of the attraction to tree houses—to try out crazy ideas and be an uninhibited kid again?

FAVORITE FEATURES

I love the slab siding on this one, and truth be told, I usually don't adore slab siding. However, these log sides can often be obtained for free or for very little from lumber mills, so they are definitely something to consider. I've seen people work wonders with them, but just note that since they are a nonstandard size and quality, they can sometimes be a little more challenging to work with.

The rustic and salvaged windows are just great looking in addition to being a money saver. This tree house reminds us to think beyond the parameters of the norm, to look to everyday objects that could be turned into windows, such as front-loading washing machine doors and IKEA thick plastic storage container lids (things that I have used). Sometimes it pays to get "weird."

And the suspension bridge adds to the overall fun. While a bit challenging to build, it gives the immediate feel that one is about to enter a very unconventional space. It sets the stage.

EDELWEISS
TREE HOUSE

DEFYING THE OLD SAYING that "Everything is bigger in Texas" is this tiny—but big on style—tree house built by Klint Kuykendall. Built on posts to fit (almost hover) within a small pocket of tree limbs, this minute hideout had to be kept on the narrow side (it's barely over 4 feet wide). Like any good hideout, it is tough to spot from afar, enveloped by the surrounding tree limbs and foliage.

Building within the confines of a tree while doing one's best not to alter or eliminate parts of the tree can often be a challenge. Kuykendall met that challenge brilliantly, creating a structure that looks as if it were meant to be there. And while narrow rooms, excepting hallways, won't often work in residential homes, in the tree house world one gets a "hall pass" (weak pun intended), as small and cozy spaces provide an outside-the-norm experience.

LOCATION: Gruene, Texas

SIZE: 64 square feet

BUDGET: $$

DESIGNER/BUILDER: Klint Kuykendall

AMENITIES: Electricity

EDELWEISS
TREE HOUSE
continued

With its great sense of style and some very attractive board-and-batten siding (sourced from cedar fence pickets to keep costs down), this is one darn cool clubhouse that would be a dream come true for any kid. A spot like this could also make for a rather amazing office space with a simple built-in desk and some wall shelves. On the other hand, the view and vibe might be both too relaxing and distracting to get any work done.

FAVORITE FEATURE

This tiny Dutch-style tree house would be more of a Dutch oven were it not for the plentitude of operable awning windows (salvaged from an old farmhouse), each of which can be quickly pushed open and propped up with a simple built-in toggle stick. These little functional hacks—very simple and often unnoticed—are almost genius.

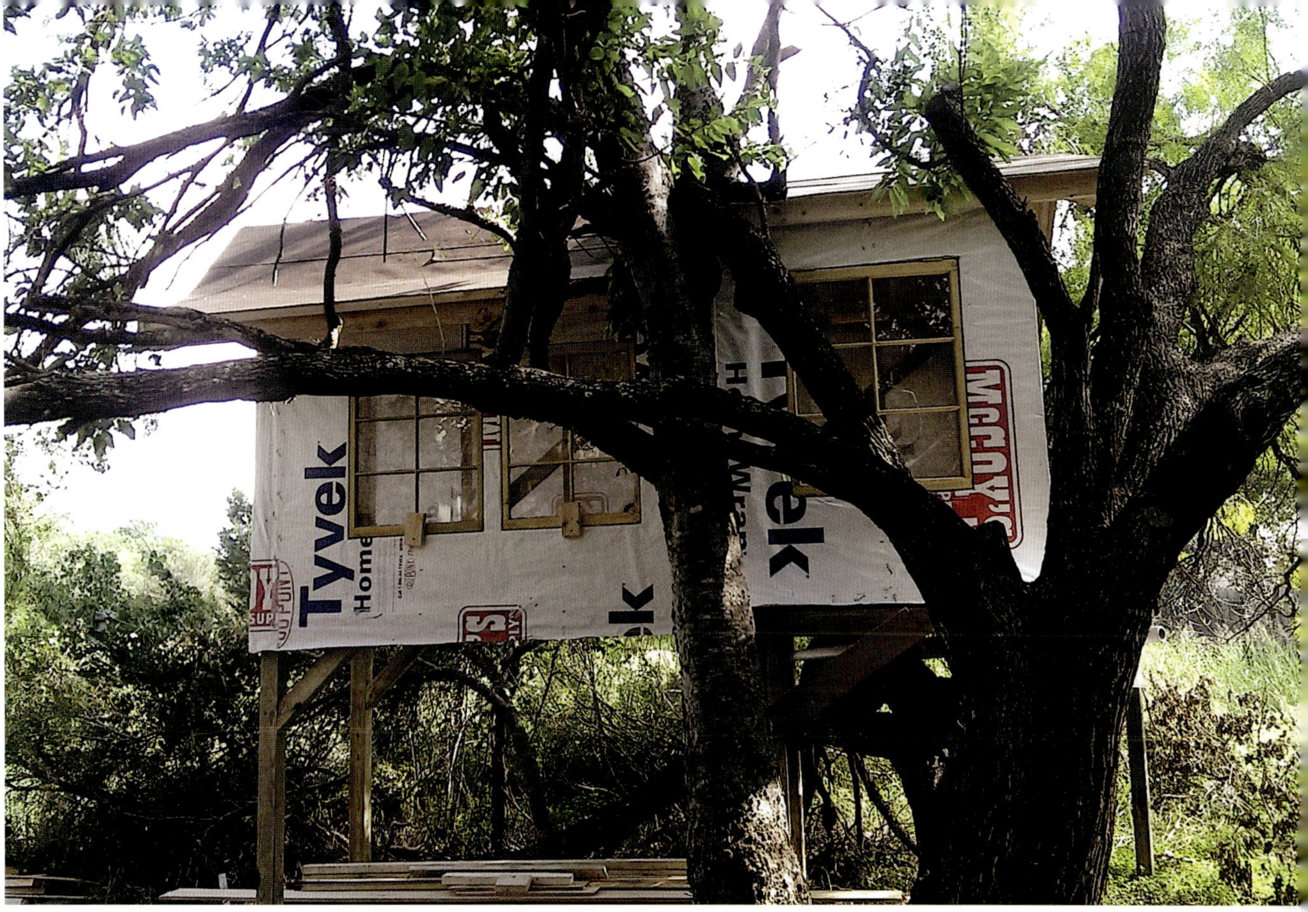
Tyvek
Home

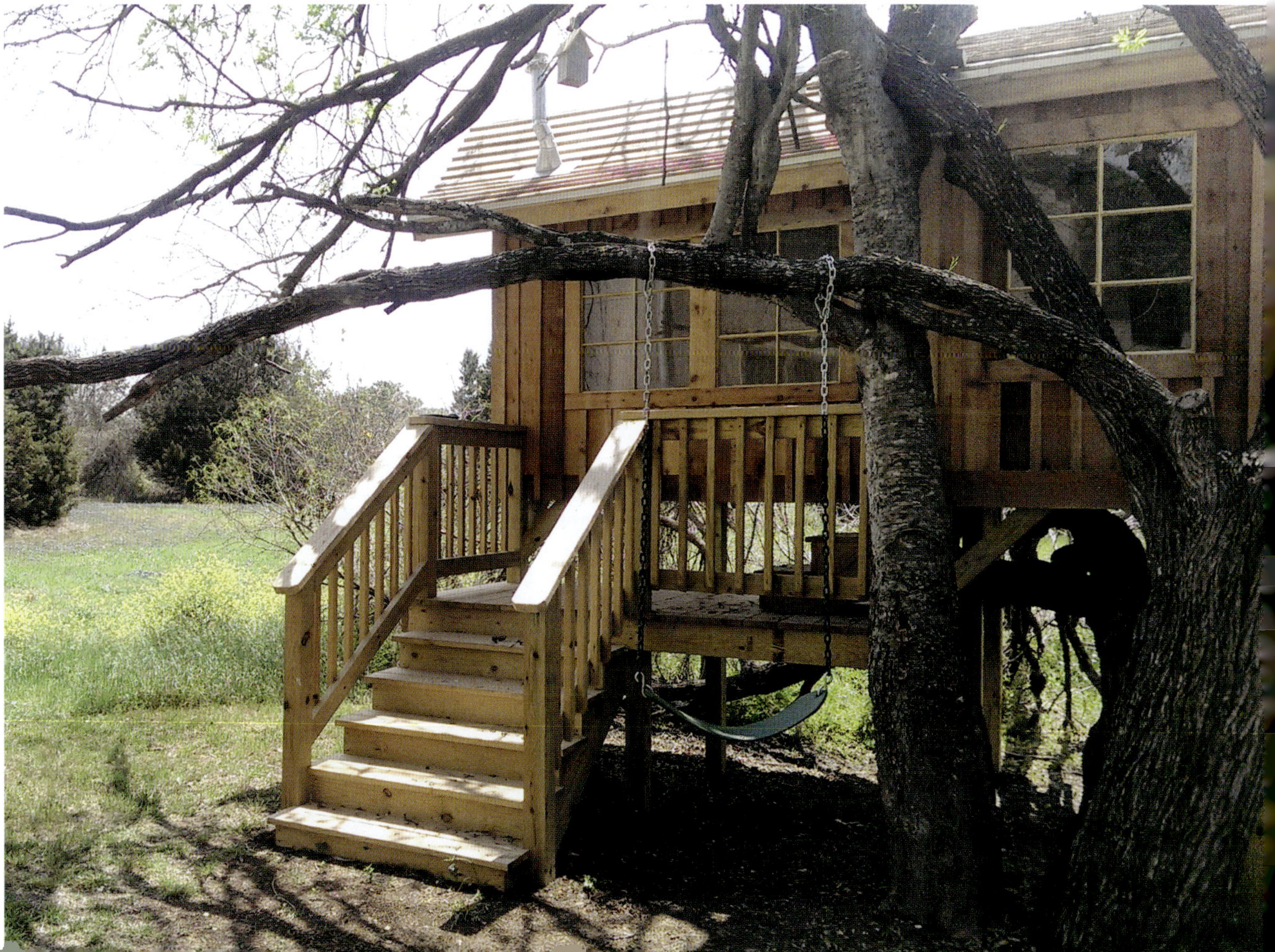

ARTISTIC
TREE HOUSE

BUILT FOR ONLY a few hundred dollars by using salvaged and repurposed materials and milling local materials, this Danish tree house was created with the intention of being rented out to guests. And rented out it has been—several hundred people have rented it on Airbnb.

A true, pole-less tree house, it is located a hair higher than 12 feet up in the air and held aloft by one single tree. With its sweeping ladderlike stairs, large skylight wall for stargazing, and natural curvilinear railings, it has funkiness and overall cool factor in spades. It even has a little deck, complete with two chairs and a tiny little cocktail table where guests can relax outdoors.

Inside, it is only large enough to fit one small double bed with a little luggage storage to spare. Built-in shelves line the walls, some provided by the horizontal framing of the tree house's sides. And while it may look like a teeter-totter accident waiting to topple, it is incredibly strong and lightweight, built to ensure that it lasts.

LOCATION: Eskilstrup, Denmark

SIZE: 42 square feet

BUDGET: $ (most wood milled on site)

DESIGNER/BUILDER: Flemming Rasmussen

AMENITIES: Small woodstove and separate bathhouse

FAVORITE FEATURES

This tree house is artistic indeed. None of its corners seem perfectly square, the deck is somewhat amorphic in shape, and the twisting ascent up to the structure comes off as an adventure in itself, perfectly setting the stage for the unconventional vibe within.

The window that continues upward into the ceiling as a skylight really opens up this tiny tree house interior. Skylights can be cheaply fabricated and often lend space, light, ventilation, and even egress to any tree house. It's also rather amazing and soothing to sleep under a large tree house skylight when it's raining.

ARTISTIC
TREE HOUSE
continued

I'm a big fan of bright colors, but this one doesn't need them at all. The intricate and seemingly random patterns and eccentricities of the locally milled lumber are eye-catching all on their own.

And this rental isn't without amenities, either. A very charming bathroom cabin with a toilet and shower, built solely for this tree house, awaits below, though going down those ladder steps in the middle of the night might be a hair perilous. This tree house also features a small woodstove should the nights get too chilly.

Guests at this cool tree house can drink a cocktail while checking out the view from the deck, then sleep below the skylight.

RAY
OF
SUNSHINE
TREE HOUSE

LOCATION: Roseburg, Oregon

SIZE: 110 square feet (including deck)

BUDGET: $$$

DESIGNER/BUILDER: Hunter Kekoa Bancroft (Breathe Easy Treehouses)

AMENITIES: None (fresh air and natural light)

BUILT IN THE WOODS of Oregon, the Ray of Sunshine tree house was both a passion and a tribute project. The only requirement from its owner was that a single gallon of green paint be used in its building. The paint had been given to the owner by her dear friend Mary, with the intention of it being used on the owner's future tree house. Mary, who was like a ray of sunshine to those who knew her, sadly died of cancer at far too young an age.

This artist studio was crafted to be an open space with a wealth of light for painting. It employs a simple one-pitch roof that doubles in one quadrant as a skylight through its use of clear Suntuf polycarbonate. In a sense, roof and window here become one. It's also a very cost-effective and time-saving approach.

Safety Note

Placing the entry point (the bridge) of this tree house on the low side makes good sense, as it is safer and easier to access during the construction phase (less ladder work and at safer heights). For these reasons, I would build the deck and bridge first before putting up a single stick of the structure itself.

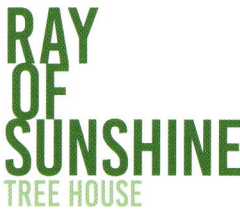

RAY
OF
SUNSHINE
TREE HOUSE

continued

Nestled in a big white oak on a hillside, this tree house doesn't look very high off the ground at its entry (8 feet), but as one descends downhill and takes a look from another position, it soon appears almost towering in height with a 15-foot vantage.

Beyond its inspiring backstory, this studio in the trees is also a very impressive offering from a first-time builder, from its attention to detail to the fact that it stands as a true tree house with not a single earthbound pole holding it up. Even its windows were built from scratch—something few builders would take the time and hassle to tackle. And the 20-foot-long suspension bridge that travels from the hillside to the low end of the tree house (8 feet in the air) isn't anything to scoff at, either. These bridges take a healthy combination of time, money, and skill to produce. Few could wish for a more flattering or heartfelt tribute.

THIS ARTIST STUDIO WAS CRAFTED TO BE AN OPEN SPACE WITH A WEALTH OF LIGHT FOR PAINTING.

RAY
OF
SUNSHINE
TREE HOUSE
continued

(Top) The clear Suntuf roofing also doubles as a source of natural light— almost all of the roof becomes a skylight.

(Bottom) Here is a great example of tree house TAB hardware put to use.

THE
BROCKTON
BOX

THE
BROCKTON
BOX
continued

LOCATION: Brockton, Massachusetts

SIZE: 58 square feet

BUDGET: $$

DESIGNER/BUILDER: Derek "Deek" Diedricksen

AMENITIES: None

I WAS ASKED TO BUILD this particular structure as a birthday present for a boy who was very into tree houses (I mean, most kids are, right?). "Small but mighty" was my aim, as the budget at hand was fairly meager.

The goal of the project soon became finding ways to spruce up a basic box, so that it would feel like much more than that. I largely did this by using several clear Sunlite Multiwall sheets as wall panels. These not only saved a bit of time and money, but they also made the entire build a bit lighter, which was of key importance, as I prefabricated the structure and had to carry every piece to the site. The clear walls also opened things up and ultimately made it feel less like a shipping crate.

"SMALL BUT MIGHTY" WAS MY AIM.

THE
BROCKTON
BOX
continued

While there wasn't enough money in the budget to build a deck overlooking the gorgeous one-acre pond, I created that vibe by recycling an enormous panel from a sliding glass door for a direct water view, and additionally crafted a swing-open panel/window with a railing—much like a lo-fi Juliette balcony. The result was an unobstructed view of the pond and a ton of fresh air if this greenhouse-like cabin ever got too warm.

As for other aspects, I added a mini sleep loft or play bunk and gave a second life to a bunk bed ladder I found free on the side of the road. I also gave the tree house a little triangular landing at its entrance, reached by an easy-to-climb set of stairs. Stairs (as opposed to a ladder) are always easier for the builder and for the future occupants.

GHISLETTI
TREE HOUSE

This tree house, designed by Michele Ghisletti for her kids, is an amalgam of simplicity and elegance. Yes, it has a boxlike shape, but on further inspection one starts to notice the details that make it so attractive.

The arched doorway adds elegance, and the exterior stain makes the structure look refined. And the cantilevered pulley-and-bucket rigging, the inset chessboard floor, and the fold-down wall table all show that there is more to the matter than what you see at first glance.

LOCATION: Brignano, Italy

SIZE: 64 square feet

BUDGET: $$

DESIGNER/BUILDER:
Michele Ghisletti

AMENITIES: LED/solar lights

As with many tree houses, the large windows open up this small space, making it feel larger, but they also provide the parents with a view of their kids in this case, so they can keep an eye on them from inside the house. I've had parents ask for large windows in the tree house for this very reason.

THE ARCHED DOORWAY ADDS ELEGANCE, AND THE EXTERIOR STAIN MAKES THE STRUCTURE LOOK REFINED.

GHISLETTI
TREE HOUSE
continued

While Ghisletti's backyard didn't have any trees that would support the house, she was able to place the posted house within the hug of a tree and its branches. I call this the next-best-thing approach. It works. The gnarled look of this small backyard tree adds to the overall interest of this tree house as well.

And one final note: If you're building in a residential area, a more traditionally shaped structure like this might go over better with nearby neighbors. Always keep in mind that others may be forced to look at your tree house from their own windows. The last thing you want is bad neighborly relations, or, even worse, your neighbors calling in building inspectors in an attempt to shut down your project or force you to remove it. It has happened.

The pulley door is a fun touch. It helps open the door in awninglike fashion and can be tethered down to hold it open as well.

FAVORITE FEATURES

What I love most about this tree house is its simplicity. It's another build that goes to show that you don't need a team of architects, a $40,000 budget, and a crew of carpenters to make something that is not only aesthetically appealing but outright magical and fun for both kids and adults. I often appreciate these scaled-back tree houses more than the extravagant ones. I call them "keeping it real" tree houses—real cheap! The little metal squirrel affixed to the exterior is a nice, fun touch, too.

Note the wall-stored craft table here in usage mode. You can see how it tucks away and saves space on the opposite page. I personally might even go so far as to attach an art piece to its underside so that It's even more clandestine in storage mode—in effect, a secret table.

GHISLETTI
TREE HOUSE
continued

The rock retaining wall under the tree house is another nice above-and-beyond touch. It looks great and adds another zone for imaginative play. It could also be used as an attractive garden bed if filled with soil.

STONE CITY
TREE HOUSE

AS THE OLD SAYING GOES, "Location, location, location!" The Stone City Tree House manages to firmly hit it out of the park in that department. This is immediately evident as you walk down the trail leading to this tiny home nestled next to a creek at the foot of the Green Mountains in Vermont.

LOCATION: Hardwick, Vermont

SIZE: 240 square feet (additional 90 with foyer and deck)

BUDGET: $$$$

DESIGNERS/BUILDERS: Heather Davis and The Treehouse Guys, LLC

AMENITIES: Indoor kitchen with running water, composting toilet, shower at main residence, electric heat

STONE CITY
TREE HOUSE
continued

Take one quick look around and you'll spot a firepit that is on the very precipice of the creek's edge, a giant triangular hammock that takes full advantage of the outdoor setting by being planted partially over the edge of the water, and then there is one of the house's coolest features: the open-air swing bed. "Wow! This place is awesome!" exclaimed one of my kids, completely running past the tree house and making a beeline to the river hammock. I rest my case.

"WOW! THIS PLACE IS AWESOME!" EXCLAIMED ONE OF MY KIDS.

Built as a labor of love in 2017 to expand a rental business, the Stone City Tree House is charm galore within. A wraparound couch, a snug little loft accessible by ladder, and a very spacious outdoor deck make this place so very usable. There's no running for an outhouse down a long trail at night, as this tree house even has its own indoor composting toilet room (with a window for ventilation—important!). But the focal point of this entire indoor experience would have to be its tiny, fun, well-thought-out kitchen. Here single mom and owner Heather Davis cranks up the charm by making such a small space functional and appealing. And the intentional positioning of the windows to give a 180-degree view of the creek certainly doesn't hurt, either. As small as this kitchen is, Davis makes it a place you want to be in. And how many tree houses manage to fit in a sectional couch *and* a mini electric fireplace? Both comfort and style are certainly in harmony in this mere 240 square feet of treetop heaven.

(Top) While the loft isn't exactly ultraspacious, it's fun, saves space down below, and has a heck of a view of the river and forest below.

(Bottom) The kitchen—and even the little bathroom nook with its composting toilet—are not only functional but inviting as well. They have both a sense of country charm and a more free-spirited aesthetic.

While the Stone City Tree House stands as one of the pricier tree houses in this collection, there is zero doubt that Davis and The Treehouse Guys (also hosts of a show on the Magnolia Network) accomplished what they set out to create, and with great success. Booked out almost nonstop, this is a place you should try to rent far, far in advance—another testament to the burgeoning popularity of tree building.

Safety Notes

While building next to fast-moving creeks or rivers might sound like a great idea, be mindful of flooding. Carefully consider how high the water will rise in the wet season, eventual erosion, and the root system and strength of trees in close proximity to the water (the trees here were not very close to the stream bank). Rapid waters also tend to be very loud, and while they can serve as white noise to some, aiding with a good night's rest, others may find the noise too loud for sleep. Good windows and insulated walls will certainly help muffle the clamor, should you need to do so.

SCHAARSBERGEN

TREE HOUSE

I JUST LOVE the sophisticated simplicity of this tree house in the Netherlands, with its asymmetrical shingles, clunky 'n' chunky slab siding, and dual-level presentation. And the beauty of it is that this tree house looks more complicated and intricate than it actually is—none of its features require anything near rocket science to build.

Take, for example, designer Bijl's decision to keep what to some might seem like a cumbersome, troublesome, and space-wasting tree branch. I know I would have been tempted to cut it down myself. But by leaving it intact, it becomes a very interesting and unique part of the structure. It also directly reminds people they are up in a tree, enhancing this unique and novel experience.

LOCATION:
Schaarsbergen,
the Netherlands

SIZE: 161 square feet

BUDGET: $$$$$

DESIGNER/BUILDER:
Menno Bijl/Bijl
Boomhutten

AMENITIES: None

SCHAARSBERGEN
TREE HOUSE

continued

A branch like this could also provide a place to sit, or become a place to hang a swing seat or lanterns. One could even affix a few level and horizontal boards atop it here and there to serve as scattered shelves. A side product of building around existing branches is that you add all these cool little breeze holes and micro windows in the walls, adding further interest. Kids love them as spy holes, too.

The little sub-deck below the tree house is also interesting. This platform is so small that it's really only usable by kids, becoming a special nook for playing. Below that (again, a case where otherwise dead space is turned into a useful area) is room to store logs for the nearby firepit.

This whole structure is held aloft by natural skinned trunks and logs. Criss-crossing braces add a touch of "fire tower stability," and Ewok Village–like ladders serve as access and there is an abundance of light and air in the interior. It's charming and rustic in the very best of ways. This guy knows his stuff.

A SIDE PRODUCT OF BUILDING AROUND EXISTING BRANCHES IS THAT YOU ADD ALL THESE COOL LITTLE BREEZE HOLES AND MICRO WINDOWS IN THE WALLS.

FAVORITE FEATURES

If you look closely, this tree house, like many from Bijl Boomhutten, has multiple avenues of access. Kids *love* this. There is the rope ladder with rungs, the natural-limb ladder to the second deck, and the climbing wall that doubles as access and entertaining activity—it seems as if the builders have thought of it all. This is also a great way of "tricking" kids into getting a little exercise.

THE
SKY
BUNGALOW

MOST TREE HOUSE NERDS will recognize the name Dustin Feider, as this guy has been making wildly creative designs for quite some time. He is pretty darn inventive and not afraid to push the envelope when it comes to bizarre builds, like this Sky Bungalow. (Also check out his zenlike Sacred Forest Tree House on page 131.)

FAVORITE FEATURES

The ocular windows add a large expense, but sometimes these little splurge extravagances are just what a build calls for. Tiny house builder Jay Shafer often preaches the same mindset when talking about the custom Gothic window he installed in his über-cheap, self-built home. This could be your one build in life—a path of sweat and long hours—so you might as well make it count.

I also appreciate how the tree was left in place as a staging piece to make this look like a tree house. Without it, it would present more as an industrial stilt house than as a tree house.

Part futuristic Conestoga wagon, part Willy Wonka alien spaceship, the Sky Bungalow is certainly one of a kind in more than a few ways. One immediately notices its unique shape and pine cone–like layered roof shingles. While most would not even bother tackling a vaulted or curved roof or an eyebrow window and ocular centerpiece that fits the curved motif of the piece, Feider seems to almost gleefully jump into these more complex approaches. And trust me, this one is simple compared to his other geometric and ultra-mathematical builds. But it's these little above-and-beyond touches that ultimately make a huge difference and lend such individualism and character to his work.

The Sky Bungalow also might stand as one of the more unusual builds by way of its supporting assemblage. With the owners wanting to retain usage of a near-dead tree trunk in their backyard, Feider crafted a custom-welded steel support cradle for the shelter itself. The steel support anchors the tree house deep into the ground, stabilizes and cradles its weight, and enables the aging stump to appear as if it is doing most of the work. It's a melding of new and old, and all with a heck of a lot of flair. Any kid would be beyond lucky to have a tree house like this.

LOCATION: Wisconsin

SIZE: 65 square feet

BUDGET: N/A

DESIGNER/BUILDER: Dustin Feider

AMENITIES: Fresh air through one really cool window

FLOATING
TREE HOUSES

WITH THEIR SEMI-DOMED OR "SHELLED" APPEARANCE, these incredibly unique works from the Belgian team Trees and People look like part UFO and part Buckminster Fuller's Dymaxion House. With one quick glance at these floating tree houses, you can see that a deep love of trees was at the heart of this design.

In alignment with the company's mission statement to pursue no-trace construction that has no negative impact on the environment, these tree houses do not penetrate or damage the trees in any way at all. They affix to the trees via an adjustable and flexible banding system. They're like an upgraded version of padded cargo straps, but instead of being used to tie down lumber to your car roof rack, these bands grasp the trees to provide attachment, or hanging, points. It's a versatile means of attaching the tents to the trees without ever permanently latching on to them or hurting them.

LOCATION: Chevetogne, Belgium

SIZE: 215 square feet

BUDGET: $$—$$$$

DESIGNERS: Bruno de Grunne and Nicolas d'Ursel of Trees and People

AMENITIES: None/off grid

FLOATING
TREE HOUSES
continued

Trees and People sells these tree houses as kits that can be put up and taken down when needed. Essentially a tree house tent with a wood floor, they are lightweight and portable. I'm not sure how these tree house support methods would cross over to the world of fully wood-framed builds, since traditional framing is so heavy compared to these tents.

I love everything about these. While I imagine they would be rather expensive for most, I think that the cost is probably fair, given all the work and engineering that goes into them. Even if you don't plan on building a tree house that approaches this scope, you might still find ideas and inspiration in the design. The one downside of these: You'd better have an abundance of trees on your lot, and big ones at that. I would also assume that while the strap-based hardware is built to last, it might not last as long as some of the steel hardware on the market. Though with tree houses in general, as with almost anything, nothing is forever.

FAVORITE FEATURE

The ability to use and then possibly relocate and reuse these attachment braces might be a huge selling point for some. Tired of one location after a few years? Well, just take down the tree house tent and move it to another locale. Trying that with a traditional bolted-in tree house would be a lot more laborious and challenging by comparison.

(Top) These tree houses are a great example of not only preserving nature, but letting the outdoors in. However, in inclement weather, they still close up nicely.

(Bottom) By being angled and extending outward, the included railings on these structures intrude less on the view of the surrounding landscape.

THE BIRD'S NEST

THIS LUXURY TREETOP EDIFICE designed and built by The Treehouse Guys lies on Bliss Ridge, a plot of family land deep in the woods of Vermont. With modern amenities and pleasant rustic touches, this tree house retains a feeling of simplicity and backwoods subtleness, while also being a fairly gigantic and extravagant build—maybe even the most extravagant in the book.

LOCATION: Moretown, Vermont

SIZE: 280 square feet (interior), 250 square feet (exterior)

BUDGET: $$$$$

DESIGNER: B'fer Roth

BUILDERS: B'fer Roth/ The Treehouse Guys, LLC/ son-in-law/wife

AMENITIES: Outdoor shower with hot water, bathroom, solar electricity, and propane heat

THE
BIRD'S
NEST
continued

As James "B'fer" Roth explains, "With the Bird's Nest, we pulled out all the stops." And the man wasn't fibbin'. This is quickly evident when you walk in and see the debarked tree limbs used to make railings and the beautiful custom ladder to the upper loft area. Having worked with natural and debarked materials before, I know firsthand how challenging it can be to craft with such asymmetrical, organic, and amorphic materials. The finished product shows how skill, time, and the simplest of materials can be combined to create a rather dramatic and amazing effect.

Another dose of "wow" is experienced when you cross the rope bridge that leads to this amazing tree home. Rope bridges can be rather time consuming and challenging to safely build, not to mention expensive. They usually necessitate the construction of another platform, another stout tree nearby for attaching an anchor to the bridge, and an abundance of materials. For that reason, most builders choose far simpler and budget-friendly options, such as ladders and traditional stairways. But one glimpse at this lamp-lit rope bridge and you can see that sometimes it *is* worth taking the high road.

I'd urge such an approach when dealing with rental tree houses, where you want to almost overwhelm and impress clients or guests from the get-go. Add the fact that walking luggage and gear across a bridge is far easier than perilously climbing a ladder with anything, and you'll start to see why some builders are so fond of the bridge route. Another idea would be to build a long access ramp to your tree house entrance, which is also advantageous for lugging materials during the building phase. Having an ADA-compliant tree house would be another great, and appreciated, rental perk.

"WITH THE BIRD'S NEST, WE PULLED OUT ALL THE STOPS," SAID BUILDER B'FER ROTH.

FAVORITE FEATURES

I love the incorporation of salvaged and vintage windows that vary in size and position, adding to the overall charm of the space.

And this gorgeous tree house even has a small kitchen—a touch of modern luxury but in a rustic and down-home way. A galvanized washtub serves as a kitchen sink in place of a stock model. It is somehow fancy without being overly flashy and showy.

I also love the wonky, crooked playhouse roof. It gives a tree house a very playful and childlike look, but it also necessitates a lot more complex and nonuniversal cuts. It can be tedious work. But for some, the mathematical challenges of angular and free-form builds such as this one are appealing and a labor of love. Those of us with less patience—and especially those who never excelled in math class—might want to opt for a more straightforward route.

THE
BIRD'S
NEST

continued

THE ATLANTA NEST

THE ATLANTA NEST (my name, not the builder's) intentionally has a very open feel. The designers wanted to make a structure that could be used by both kids and adults. The main level is an open deck where the family could hold a dinner party or gathering, while a mere 7 feet above lies the very coolest facet of this tree house—the nest itself.

LOCATION: Atlanta, Georgia, area

SIZE: 64 square feet and a netted loft, 128-square-foot deck

BUDGET: $$$$$

DESIGNER/BUILDER: Treehouse Experts

AMENITIES: None

THE
ATLANTA
NEST
continued

I've seen all sorts of net-lounge approaches, from handwoven versions to actual trawling nets for fishing boats. These affixed nets are installed more or less as room-size hammocks, and they add such an element of fun and comfort to a build. They don't block any views or enclose a space, so they're another way to make your tree house feel larger and more spacious than it is. While they do require a bit of customization (by hand or by order) and can be expensive, nets may be worth it for the "cool" element they add. Many are even comfortable enough to nap or sleep overnight on, depending on how tightly they are installed. The row of narrow windows along the side wall makes for great star viewing while lounging in the nest at night.

Safety Note

If you're going to install a rope nest and want to repurpose netting, just be sure to get a variety whose holes are not so large as to snag or trap kids. You want to be able to freely move and crawl about these webs without having to worry about hands or legs falling through (or worse—getting caught or tangled). You'll also want to pick some form of rope that doesn't stretch over time, leaving you with a rather saggy mess of a loft in the end. Plus, certain poly-based ropes fray and become abrasive, almost splintery, over time. Avoid those.

In the case of locale, this one is certainly a grand slam. As a rule of thumb, I try to build any tree house within view of a body of water, be it a stream, river, or pond. It just seems to add to the outdoorsy vibe and provides great views that make all your blood, sweat, and tears building an elevated structure with "lookout views" worth it. As you see, the builders took full advantage of their private pond and surrounding woodland acreage. If you're going to have an elevated view, always make sure you're designing it to face something beautiful where possible. I don't, however, recommend building near wetlands before talking to your local zoning commission. Just jumping into a build could open up a whole can of "code worms" that you don't want to deal with.

SACRED FOREST
TREE HOUSE

HERE'S AN EXAMPLE of effective aesthetics through simplicity. Instead of masking or covering up the house with loads of siding or synthetic materials, the designer, Dustin Feider, opted for a bare and more natural look. Here the wood itself—the very visible wall, stud, and woodwork—is put on display. Nothing is hidden beneath drywall or an abundance of paint. Feider embraces the materials that give birth to these creations. And why shouldn't he? How can we actually improve on the natural and intricate wood grain of lumber?

LOCATION: Woodside, California

SIZE: 120 square feet

BUDGET: $$$$

DESIGNER/BUILDER: Dustin Feider/O2 Treehouses

AMENITIES: Electricity (via solar power) and nearby outhouse

SACRED FOREST
TREE HOUSE
continued

There are several other noteworthy aspects of this tree house. Take, for instance, the over-the-top array of clear panels. Feider is able to keep the vibe of this space from becoming too stark, too modern, or too cold by also incorporating the natural wood and golden hue of the grains and patterns of the walls. Even with so much of the wall and ceiling work made of clear panels, somehow it's still a warm and welcoming space.

It's tightly sealed from the elements, too, with flexible trim that collars and closes the gap around the penetrating tree. And if you wanted to bring the outside in, you could simply open the sliding door. Easy to open and close, the custom slider runs on a track much like factory-built models.

This unpretentious space, ideal for meditation or yoga, is additionally kept from feeling too empty and clinical with the inclusion of a few tasteful touches, such as the small sleep loft. The loft with a cozy bed makes the space more versatile. Further, hanging chains affixed to large lag screws to support it make the tree house appear almost as if it's floating—part boat and part giant swing set seat. It has an inviting and nestlike feel even with its straight walls and hard edges.

Safety Note

Hatches protect against unwelcome guests, as you can close and latch them, and they also often save space, as the hatch becomes a portion of the deck when closed. However, I'm usually wary of tree houses accessed by hatches—I feel they can be dangerous, since you can slam your fingers in them. To mitigate this risk, Feider has wired this hatch so that it can be operated and locked open from the ground below (note the control cable/wires)—a simple but clever solution to something that might otherwise be problematic.

CARUTHERS PIRATE SHIP

THIS TREE HOUSE is certainly well out of the ordinary—not only in shape but also in scope. Truth be told, while I've seen other nautical-style tree houses, I've never seen one of this magnitude before! This enormous floating fort had to not only work itself around the site's trees but be cradled and supported by them as well. Plus every stick of lumber in this pirate ship is pressure-treated, so it's heavy, adding to the difficulty of such a build. I can't imagine how much this thing weighs!

LOCATION: Northern Michigan

SIZE: 300 square feet

BUDGET: $$$$

DESIGNER/BUILDER: Dan Wright/Tree Top Builders

AMENITIES: None

While some builders might have chosen to make the ship itself a simple, one-level, no-frills affair to cut back on materials and difficulty, this one comes out guns blazing. I particularly love the many different platforms and quadrants. All these separate spaces, crow's nests, and elevated decks make a build like this far more than its base-level layout could have been. It creates a multitude of play zones.

CARUTHERS PIRATE SHIP

continued

ADD IN THE ROPE LADDERS, SIDE HATCHES, PORTHOLES, AND THE RATHER LOFTY LOOKOUT, AND THIS ONE WOULD BE A DREAM TREE HOUSE FOR ALMOST ANY KID.

And don't forget the nooks and crannies. Every kid loves secret hiding spots and crawl spaces, and this pirate ship doesn't disappoint. A hatch in the main deck leads to the space in the bottom of the boat, which even features netted ends for open-air coolness (well, to keep the kids from falling out as well). Add in the rope ladders, side hatches, portholes, and the rather lofty lookout, and this one would be a dream tree house for almost any kid.

Had time, budget, and demand allowed, the area under the poop deck (yes, a real nautical term for a partial deck above the main deck at the stern) could have been enclosed for a rainproof clubhouse and sleepover space. I mean, it still could easily be done. That's the only thing I might change in this masterful build.

In fact, this ship would instantly make any kid's backyard *the* preferred place to hang out. And perhaps that should stand as a side word of warning: "Build a tree house that is too cool, and you're going to have neighbor kids visiting your yard nonstop!" And that's yet another reason to ensure that your tree house is beyond safe.

FAVORITE FEATURE

This pirate ship even has guns! Well, water cannons fixed to its side. With an adapted garden sprayer, a standard garden hose can be attached to these "cannons" for unlimited "ammo" usage. Talk about fun!

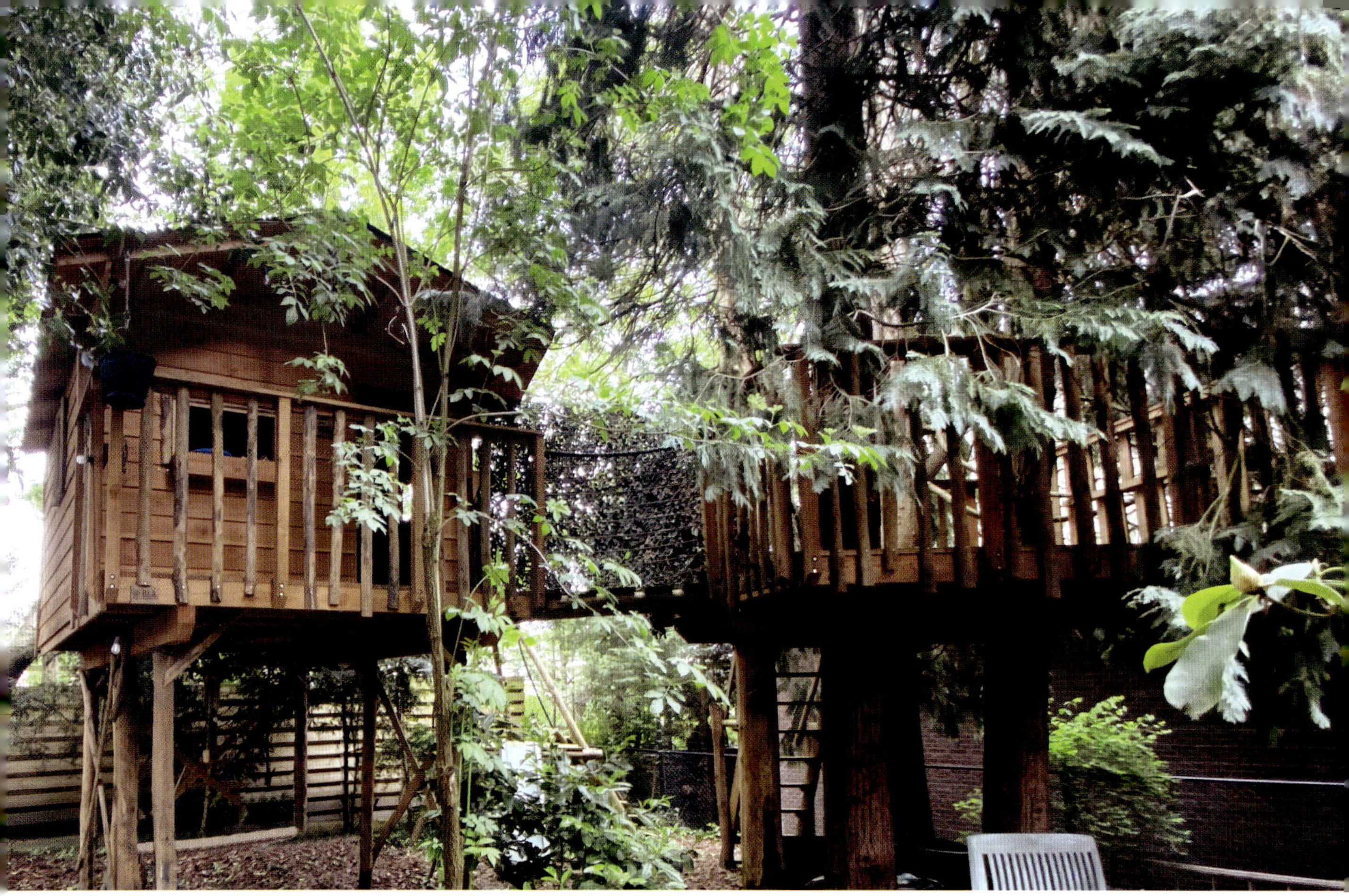

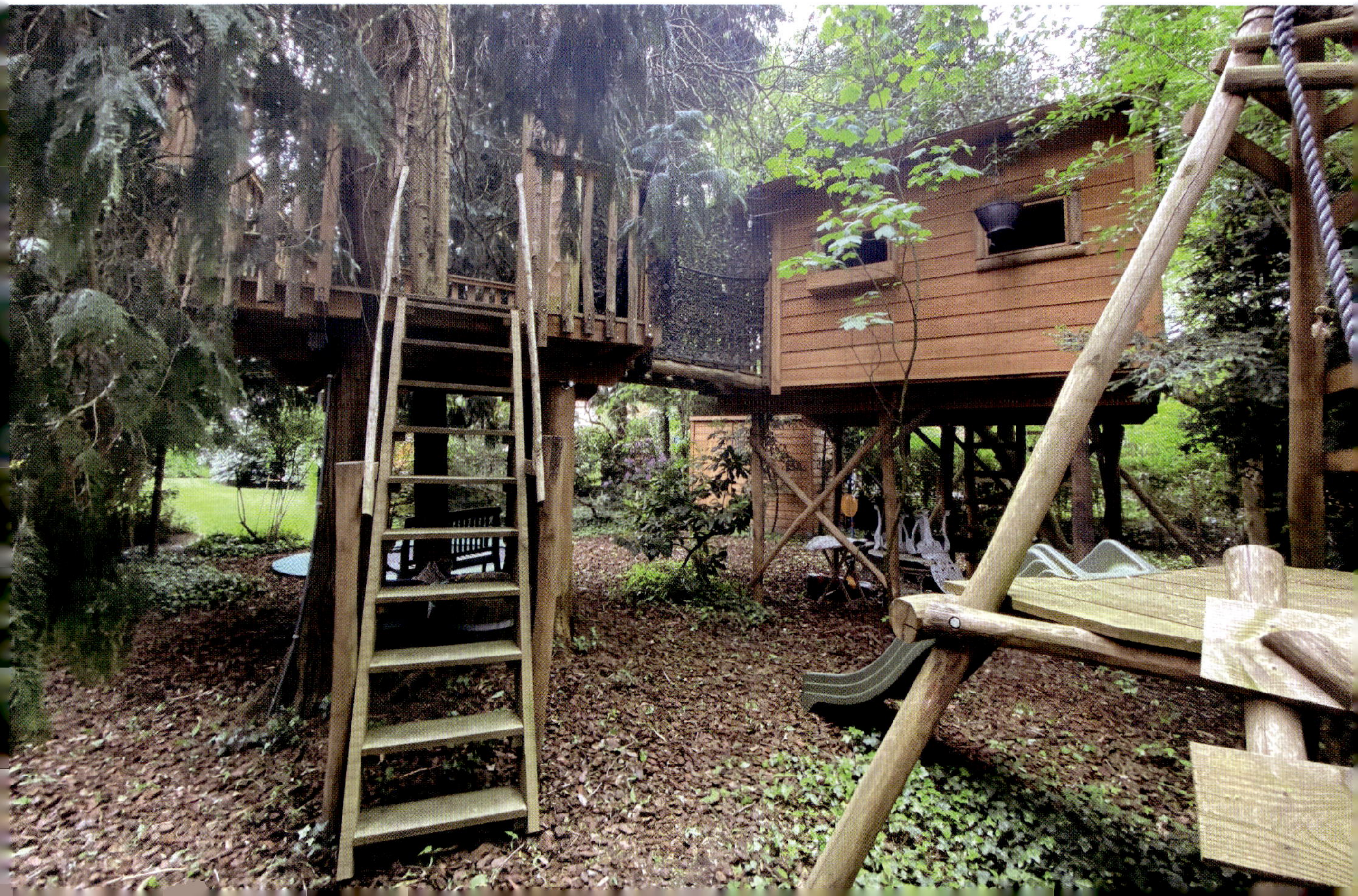

OOSTERBEEK
TREE HOUSE

THIS WORK OF BIJL BOOMHUTTEN in the Netherlands is a solid example of what I call "attractive simplicity"—clean lines, clean lumber, simple colors, and an effective and affordable design approach.

Take, for example, the simple ladder to the hatch entrance. While most people might consider building a custom ladder with chain-store lumber, or even purchasing one, Bijl built one from materials that were on site. The end product has a great rustic look and was done for zero cash outlay—penny-pinchers take note!

LOCATION: Oosterbeek, the Netherlands

SIZE: 97 square feet (with two additional decks)

BUDGET: $$$$$

DESIGNER/BUILDER: Menno Bijl/Bijl Boomhutten

AMENITIES: None

FAVORITE FEATURES

I love the built-in shelves. It's things like this that help make even the most straightforward tree houses look and feel a little more involved. I always make sure to add a few built-in features for my own clients for this very reason (we show you one of the simplest shelves that you can build on page 179). Some can even be as simple as screwing an old salvaged wooden crate or two to a wall. What was free junk collecting dust in your garage can often become not only a clever element of reuse but also a money-saving, useful item.

The secret floor/deck hatch is a fun element, too. Secret hatches and "treasure spots" are always a huge hit with kids, and that extra touch of whimsy helps make this tree house stand out.

BUILT-IN
SHELVES HELP
MAKE EVEN THE
MOST STRAIGHT-
FORWARD TREE
HOUSES LOOK
AND FEEL A
LITTLE MORE
INVOLVED.

OOSTERBEEK
TREE HOUSE
continued

Safety Notes

This is not the case with the Oosterbeek, but a universal word of warning: Be wary of using any still standing dead or cut trees for supports. They're often fine—but only for a while (and that longevity can vary by species). I've said it before but it bears repeating: Also be sure to scout your area ahead of time! Dead limbs above you *will* eventually fall.

It's also important that there is enough of a gap between deck boards for water drainage, as done with this tree house. I have seen so many decks rot out prematurely as water pools on top of the boards in heavy storms, having no place to go. Boards that are spaced but still too close together can also swell when wet, forcing the nails to pop up and break from the movement of these crowded boards. Your deck will last twice as long if you follow the simple, age-old tip to leave an adequate gap.

Like Caruthers Pirate Ship (page 134), this tree house has multiple zones in which to play. The secondary deck, accessed by a short but fun suspension bridge, gives it a far more expansive feel and allows additional space for movement. This deck also has stair access, allowing a secondary (or primary) way to get up among the trees—never a bad idea. This dual-access approach allows for circular play, too, made especially easy by the mulched surroundings down below. And the little extras like the bucket and pulley rig (almost a staple with traditional tree houses at this point) and the swing seat further add to the functionality and fun of this Bijl build.

WHISPERING WIND

TREE HOUSE

WHISPERING WIND
TREE HOUSE
continued

LOCATION: Argyle, New York

SIZE: 120 square feet and a loft

BUDGET: $$$

DESIGNERS: Victoria Cantwell and Eric Teitelbaum

BUILDERS: Eric Teitelbaum and a few of his friends

AMENITIES: Composting outhouse, propane stove and heater, battery lights

I'VE HAD THE PLEASURE of spending the night in a lot of tree houses, but the Whispering Wind Tree House, perched 15 feet in the air, was one of the most relaxing and natural. French doors on the main level opened to give way to a rather impressive and scenic expanse of farmland, something that would be more than fitting for the cover of *Country Living* magazine. Untouched by human development, the land was home to a huge array of fireflies, too (being very sensitive to pollutants, fireflies are bioindicators). The night view of them in the fields below was almost surreal.

This tree house, built to be a rental by Eric Teitelbaum (known for his work with Pete Nelson of the TV show *Treehouse Masters*) and his crew, is a great exercise in the ingenuity of using what you've got. The felled trunks of the trees that were cut down to make way for this build were used as supports for the structure. These natural posts make it look as if the tree house is entirely supported only by living trees as opposed to being a posted build. Is it a simple maneuver or thrifty and effective trickery? Whatever the case, it looks great.

THE NATURAL POSTS MAKE IT LOOK AS IF THE TREE HOUSE IS ENTIRELY SUPPORTED ONLY BY LIVING TREES.

Teitelbaum and his team further slay the money-saving game by going so far as to use long tree limbs and other discarded natural branches to assemble the entirety of this tree house's railings and knee brace supports. (These diagonal braces below the main deck give the overall structure stability through triangulation, preventing it from swaying.)

This tree house presents another great example of taking advantage of natural light by its use of polycarbonate roofing. When my kids and I spent the night here, we were given the treat of a gentle rainstorm. Because the Suntuf roofing was placed directly over the loft in the bed, it made us feel as if we were sleeping under a waterfall. The sound, the look, and the proximity of this little cascade of water was incredibly relaxing.

One other very noteworthy point of interest lies in the fact that this tree house (unlike many you'll see) manages to work in not only a small kitchenette but a functional dining table space as well—and all without making the interior space feel crowded.

Hindsight Is 20/20

It pays to talk to your neighbors and get their okay before you start building. It's just as important to know your exact land boundaries. Sadly, after a border dispute, this tree house had to be dismantled. The owners unintentionally built 30 inches beyond their property border, and the neighbor was not willing to work out an arrangement to allow this beauty to remain. But after hundreds of visitors over the years and countless memories made, it still provides us with an example of a tree house done right.

SHOE DAISY
TREE HOUSE

THE SHOE DAISY may be the single shoe that not even Shaquille O'Neal could fill. Straight out of a fairy tale, it was built for a tree house–themed adventure park in Pennsylvania called Treehouse World.

While many wouldn't rush out to build a giant boot or sneaker in their backyard—I wouldn't either, to be honest—the sheer scope and uniqueness of it is still something to marvel at. I feel it exemplifies the free-spirit mindset most tree house fans seem to have.

LOCATION: West Chester, Pennsylvania (Treehouse World)

SIZE: 140 square feet

BUDGET: $$$$$

DESIGNER/ BUILDER: Tree Top Builders

AMENITIES: None

Designed as a simple shell, or empty play space, it's a great angle-laden mathematic tree house with lots of complex cuts. It just goes to show that the sky is the limit—or close to it—in the tree house world. While perched only a half-dozen feet or so off the ground, it uses a few posts for structural support and to give it that tree house feel. When its intricate cuts and design work combine with its wild color choices, it's certainly a head turner. Much like the Robot Tree House (page 21), a build like this seems to fall within the "why the heck not?" realm. The Shoe Daisy is proof that if it can be dreamt up, it can be built—well, within reason.

Safety Notes

If you're a beginning builder, I'd stick with something far boxier and more straightforward. Angled or sloped walls are a bit cumbersome when building interior fixtures or adding furniture to any space. They are also what we call "head slammers"— a pretty self-explanatory term. They also make it tougher to add roofing and to seal the space from the elements. Do you sense a pattern of "it's not for novices" here?

PART 2

NUTS AND BOLTS

AS THE OLD saying goes, "Never put the cart before the horse." Well, the same applies to any sizable building task you're about to take on—and a tree house project would certainly fit under that banner.

For those of you new to the game, here are the general design and location considerations and a list of basic tools (most of them fairly affordable) that you might want to have in your arsenal. In this section you'll also find tips for saving money—because who doesn't want that?

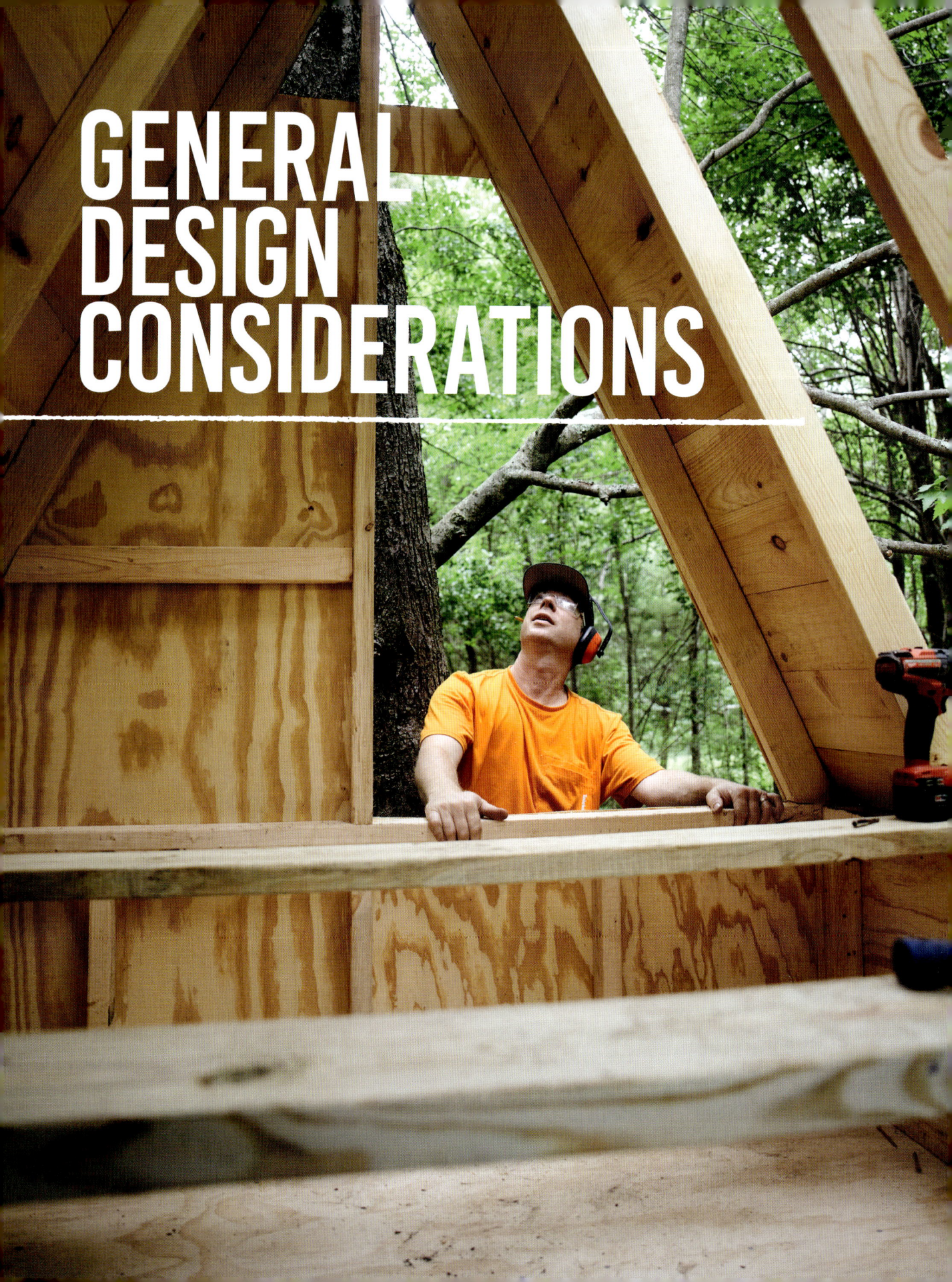

GENERAL DESIGN CONSIDERATIONS

I **COULD WRITE AN ENTIRE BOOK** on design tips and principles, but here I've gathered a few of the more straightforward, yet incredibly important, nuggets of design and layout information that I feel you should take to heart. Even if just one or two tips save you from wasted hours and money and maintain your mental well-being, you can most likely consider your cash and time with this book well spent.

THE (ABOVE) GROUND RULES

START SMALL. Or just plan to keep things smaller in general when you begin. Sure, some of you might have deeper pockets and bigger dreams and might want to hoist what amounts to a Nantucket-style home into the air (and that's all well and good!), but by starting off with a more reasonable and straightforward build, you're going to draw less attention, have fewer problems, spend less time and effort on maintenance, avoid stressing out or angering the authorities, and, well, actually be more apt to finish the thing! I highly recommend that beginners, especially, start small as you will make mistakes, which will be less costly with a tiny, basic project.

PLAN, PLAN, PLAN. If you don't, you'll waste considerable time and materials and regret it later. Sketch your ideas out, watch some YouTube videos, talk to a few pros, read this book, recommend it to friends, buy them all copies for their birthdays, give it a five-star rating . . . sorry, I got carried away. Take the time to think it out now, not in the midst of the build when you're hanging perilously from a tree and unsure about your next design move.

TAKE YOUR TIME DURING THE BUILD. Building a tree house can be dangerous. It also takes quite a bit more time than other builds you might attempt. Positioning and repositioning ladders over and over, setting up rigging, and installing walls, roofing, and, well, anything well above the ground is a recipe for injury. Be careful, take your time, and always have a cell phone in your pocket should you need help. It's also a very good idea to have someone around to watch you and assist.

GET DECENT GEAR. Don't use some bespoke, antique wooden apple-picking ladder you grabbed from a yard sale. Those are great for hanging ornamental bath towels, not for supporting your weight 12 feet off the ground.

BUILD FROM HOME. If you're building off-site, I can't stress enough how valuable it is to build as much as you can from your own yard or garage, where you have all the comforts of home. When I build for clients, I prefabricate as much of the tree house as I can at my home outside of Boston and trailer it to its final residence. For instance, I often build the panelized walls and loft, if applicable, at my home. A benefit of smaller tree houses is that when built in increments under 7 or 8 feet, most of these pieces can be attached to even the most basic of utility trailers. My Subaru (named "Dirty Larry," as it's always a construction mess) has been pulling my trailer, a mere 4 by 8 feet, for 20 years now.

⋀ AVOID TINY TREES. I try not to build on or into trees narrower than 12 inches in diameter when I can help it. Sure, you might be able to get away with smaller trees for tinier and lighter tree houses, but don't push your luck. A dogwood with a 4-inch trunk isn't going to cut the mustard. If you have a dearth of suitable backyard trees, a pole-based build (there are many showcased in this book) might be more your thing.

USE HARDWOOD TREES. Sure, other species can work—especially if they are larger and older trees (and there are still variables with these)—but hardwoods such as maples and oaks are usually the tried-and-true way to go. When in doubt, consult with an arborist; because trees are their life, they know them inside and out.

LET THOSE TREES BREATHE! Don't collar in trees too tightly with your decking or your interior tree house floor if a tree passes through the structure. These trees will widen as they grow and will sway in storms. The trees will win, you will lose, and you will then be sad. Tight collaring can hurt the trees, too—the very trees that hold up your entire build!

ASK FOR HELP. There is nothing wrong with asking for help. Sure, most people love the bragging rights of claiming "I did every single part of this build all by myself," but for every proud braggart there are a few people who got injured along the way trying to lift too much, climb too high, or do too much. I have friends with missing fingers and broken backs who can vouch for this tip.

> **USE TABS.** Be sure to build your tree house and its supporting base so that it can ride out the movement of the trees that hold it up. While each array of trees that holds up a tree house is vastly different, which makes it difficult to lay out one single set of repetitive and specific approaches, most builders use special hardware called TABs (tree house attachment bolts) to address this issue. These hardware brackets allow for the tree house and the trees to move independently of one another, all without pulling apart the trees or the build that they support. Some lower-built tree houses attached to stout trunks can get away without using TABs, and some people have hung their tree houses from chains or come up with their own welded hardware, but TABs are the most widely used approach these days.

TAKE THE LEAN OF THE TREE INTO CONSIDERATION.
Even the straightest trees have a lean (usually toward the sun). Be sure to know where that lean is so that when you build your platform, your vertical wall won't rub or bind against that tree trunk. Give the tree room to grow (a foot or so if possible, although this will vary by site and situation) and room to sway so that it won't damage the edge of your roof or your side walls.

DON'T BUILD HIGHER THAN YOU REALLY HAVE TO.
Some people want to set their build 50 feet in the air. This, I feel, adds unnecessary complications, ladder work, and structural challenges. Going "super high" will up your risk, hassle, and future injury potential. A tree house that is a mere 10 feet in the air still feels like a tree house. A tree house that is 50 feet up will take more of a beating in high winds, will require more maintenance (and difficult rope/rigging and ladder work to construct), and might require a new change of underwear for some folks when they climb to it. Unless you really yearn to feed condors by hand, you need not build something so lofty.

LOVE THY NEIGHBOR (OR AT LEAST PRETEND TO).
Make sure your neighbors are fine with your upcoming edifice. Talk to them and explain your plans before you end up with larger and costlier problems down the road if the tree house is something that encroaches on their view. This is one of the reasons that I urge clients to pick a build site as far away from their neighbors' view as possible. "Out of sight, out of mind."

LET THE MATERIALS DICTATE THE BUILD.
If you find a really cool vintage Gothic church window, or some other great salvaged element, start with that focal point and design around it, or at least don't be afraid to work it in. It's elements like these that will give your tree house individuality and make it stand out from the pack.

engineers if you are tackling a rather massive tree house. Better safe than sorry. And if you plan on renting it out, definitely look into whether or not that is allowed in your area.

◀ MAKE OVERHANGS. They help protect the outside walls of the tree house from rain. Water will break down and discolor wood over time. Overhangs are also especially effective over entrance doors—you're not getting doused with rainwater as you fumble for the tree house keys. Though, I should caution you that too large a cantilevered overhang can result in problems in high winds, as they leave too much exposed surface for upward drafts to catch onto. You don't want your roof peeling off in a big storm. Swedish architecture in snow-heavy areas has long relied on large roof overhangs; time-tested, they do work.

DON'T OVERDIVIDE A SPACE. Obviously, a divided space almost always feels smaller. When partitions are needed, pull curtains can be used in some scenarios. Curtains usually won't do when including a bathroom, so divide away!

KEEP THE ROOF SIMPLE. You don't have to get all fancy with multiple dormers if you want a quicker, easier, and more affordable build that will still look good. Single-pitch or shed roofs work well. Keep it simple if keeping it cheap is your goal.

ADD ONE POP. You don't always have to cover every exterior wall with expensive and time-consuming cedar shingles. Sometimes applying them to only one wall—a pop of fanciness—will go just as far. This is a great strategy if you have a limited amount of siding and still want things to look great. Obviously, you would want to install this "pop" wall by the entrance or on the side you first see when you approach the tree house to give it the attention it deserves.

TALK TO THE EXPERTS. This isn't a step-by-step book on how to build a tree house, and I do advise that you consult those more knowledgeable than you in certain fields if you have doubts or questions. Arborists, for example, can more accurately gauge the health and strength of a tree than most of us can—regardless of how many YouTube videos we've watched. The same goes for structural

⋀ CHOOSE STAIRS OVER LADDERS. Not only are they safer and easier to climb, but stairs don't hurt the arches of your feet as rungs do if you were to climb to a loft barefoot or in socks. Ladders are easier and less costly to build, however, and they often require fewer materials, so some might still opt for them.

USE PLYWOOD FLOORS. Plank floors look great, but without a subfloor, they will expand and contract over time and often leave gaps between each board (think: bugs, loss of heat, and drafts). Plywood floors are an easy and affordable solution (where the subfloor and floor are one and the same). Use ¾-inch plywood, though! Anything thinner will bounce too much or, even worse, won't support you at all. Tongue-and-groove wood is another option, but it's usually costlier.

⋀ MAKE HOMEMADE SKYLIGHTS. Using a sheet of Suntuf polycarbonate is a great way to install a simple and cheap large skylight at a fraction of the price of manufactured units. It is basically a microcosm of a greenhouse ceiling. That natural light will go far to open up your interior and make it a much more cheerful space.

BUILD A LANDING. It provides swing space for a door and can also break up the often two-dimensional look of an otherwise flat tree house wall. Remember to also account for your door's swing space when it comes to any built-ins and furnishings.

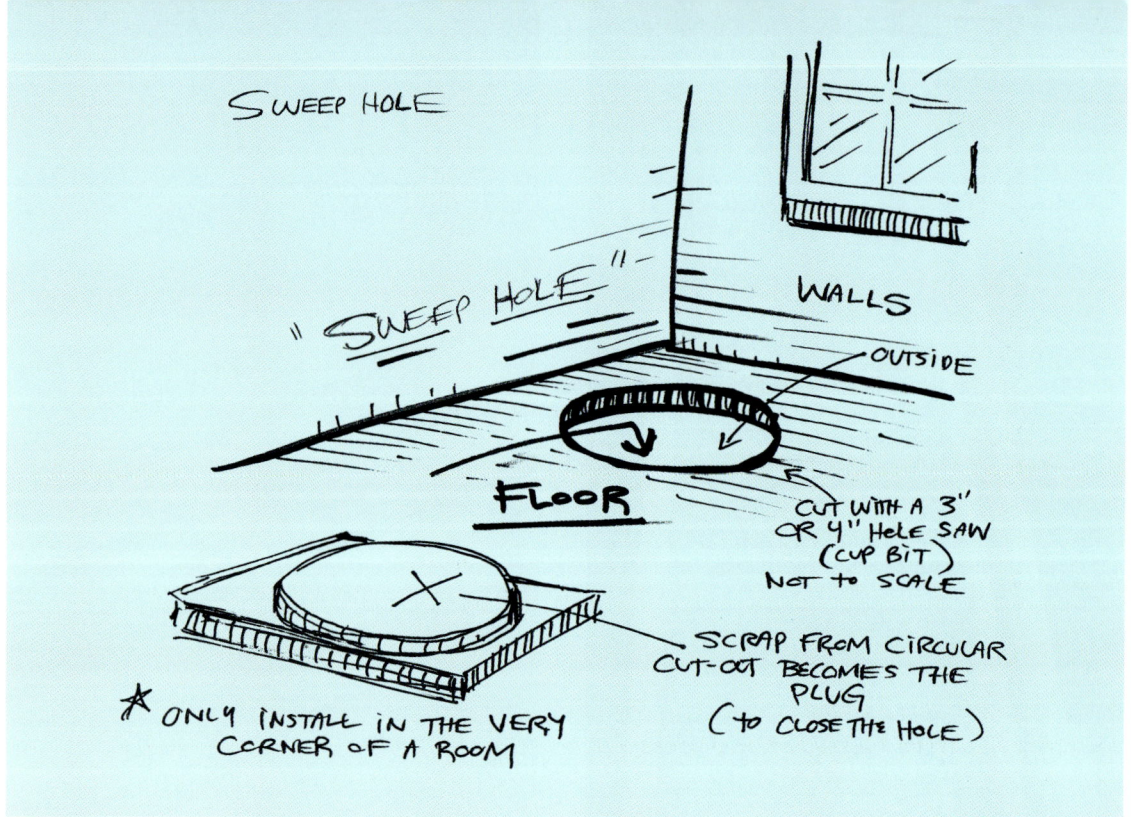

SWEEP HOLE

"SWEEP HOLE"

WALLS

OUTSIDE

FLOOR

CUT WITH A 3"
OR 4" HOLE SAW
(CUP BIT)
NOT to SCALE

SCRAP FROM CIRCULAR
CUT-OUT BECOMES THE
PLUG
(to CLOSE THE HOLE)

★ ONLY INSTALL IN THE VERY
CORNER OF A ROOM

⚠ INSTALL A SWEEP HOLE. This idea, to which I added a twist of my own, comes from David and Jeanie Stiles's fantastic book *Rustic Retreats: A Build-It-Yourself Guide.* Simply drill a 4-inch hole in a floor corner, add a square of wood with one pivoting screw in a corner of it, and each time you sweep your floors you can just swivel the "lid" open and push the debris through this hole to the ground below. It saves you from all that dustpan work. Alternatively, you can make a simple plug from the 4-inch piece you cut out and a larger scrap of wood glued to it.

CHOOSE SCREWS OVER NAILS WHEN APPROPRIATE. Most times I prefer screws over nails. They can be easily backed out or reversed when mistakes are made. Each has their advantage in certain situations, though.

USE YOUR BED FOR SEATING. Set your bed (if you have one) at a height so that it doubles as seating. The age-old concept of a daybed works and saves space, time, and money. Use the space below it for storage, too. Simple roll-out storage boxes (which can be made from discarded wooden dresser drawers with added casters) work really well. A simple curtain can conceal what is stored beneath the bed, hiding any clutter.

BUILD THE DECK RIGHT. Be sure to space those exterior deck boards to give them room for expansion and for drainage. Also, do not use finishing nails to secure your decking. Those nails always seem to work their heads up and out over time. We call those nails "screamers" from the reaction they create when you snag your bare foot on one of them. I'd go with exterior hex-head deck screws.

AVOID PHILLIPS SCREWS. If you have a choice, buy hex-head or star-head screws. The bit will be far less likely to slip off the receiving head of the screw. This choice will save your sanity. Take it from a guy who used Phillips screws for far too long because I had a free abundance of them— the hassle they created wasn't worth the money they saved me.

> **USE SWINGS AS SEATS.** These save space, are fun to sit in, and can be easily built (or you can order woven hammock seats). When you don't need or want them as seating, you can clip them against a nearby wall or take them down from their hooks. They are lightweight, too. You can make a very simple swing by boring two holes near the end of a 24-inch cut of 2×8 lumber and running a rope through these holes. The rope ends are then attached to large eye screws on a supportive joist or strong girder above.

REALIZE THE TREE HOUSE WON'T LAST FOREVER.

I hate to be the buzzkill of the party and mention this, but it's something I state to each and every person for whom I have designed. Tree houses, just like the trees they sit in, will not last forever. However, with proper care and maintenance, you can certainly get a heck of a lot of life out of them. I own a few tree houses of my own, many a decade or so old, and while some of these even employ the older lag screw (a giant wood screw with a hex head) support method, they're still doing just fine. I put in the work, I keep an eye on them, and if I see any problems in the works, I take care of them. The tree house in my front yard has been through a couple of hurricanes now and still proudly stands (also because I didn't build it 50 feet in the air).

SAFETY TIPS WHEN BUILDING FOR KIDS

DON'T BUILD HIGHER THAN 8 FEET. If a kid were to fall from such a height, chances are they wouldn't have any serious injuries.

MULCH HEAVILY. If falls were to occur, then there would be some cushioning. This is the code for playgrounds in many states; it's a good idea to look up your local codes.

RAILINGS ARE A MUST. Small sleep and play lofts in tree houses are a fun addition to what might be an otherwise plain and boring open space, but much like with exterior decks, just make sure they have safety railings of some sort. If you're dealing with very young kids, make sure the balusters are spaced less than 3½ inches apart, so that children can't get their heads stuck between them.

HATCHES MEAN STITCHES. Hatches often don't stay open when passing through them, becoming head slammers and finger smashers. There are ways to design around these risks, but generally I just avoid the hatch approach for kids.

AVOID PROTRUDING FEATURES. These lead to headaches—literally. If it's pointy and could poke someone in the eye or face, it probably will. If there's a sharp corner that someone could bang their head on—yep, they probably will.

REALLY YOUNG KIDS AND GLASS DON'T MIX. This is especially true with low-placed panes. Leaning against these glass windows won't usually result in fun fairy-tale outcomes. This is one of the reasons why I often use Suntuf or Sunlite Multiwall panels, made from flexible polycarbonate, instead.

HAVE MORE THAN ONE EXIT. Make sure there is more than one way to get out of a tree house if need be—even if it's just a flip-open window. Little kids shouldn't be playing with matches, but still, accidents happen.

USE CAUTION WITH ZIP LINES. Kids love zip lines from high tree house launches, but do you know who else loves them? Doctors. And these doctors are more than willing to bill you for the injuries your young one might sustain. Zip lines are fun—I love them—but make sure they're safely installed. Often, the tree at either end should be padded as well.

SELECTING
YOUR
SITE

YOU DON'T WANT TO haphazardly plop your tree house in any old spot. Trust me. You're going to spend quite a bit of time, money, and energy on a tree house, so you might as well do it right from the get-go. If you want to give your tree house a shot at lasting, here are a few things you might consider.

PROPER TREES. Again, hardwoods—healthy ones—are usually the safest bet, though your region might have other good options. Consider talking to someone more knowledgeable than yourself when it comes to trees and determining their species, health, and overall durability. Trees are very resilient, but some are more prone to damage and breakage than others, especially the faster-growing varieties. Trees are often the entire support system of your build, so choose wisely. I try not to attach to any tree less than 12 inches in diameter where possible, but it all depends on

the situation or build. There isn't a "one size fits all" when it comes to tree houses. See Affixing Your Tree House to the Trees (page 170) for more information.

WETLANDS. While it may be attractive in a visual sense to position your tree house on wetland regions where other buildings might not be possible or fitting, these parcels of land are just as they are named—wet. Wet and saturated soil often results in unstable root systems in trees. These trees are much more apt to tip over and be uprooted in high winds. Now add a substantial amount of weight on them and a flat surface that can act as a sail in heavy winds (your tree house walls) and you're possibly overtaxing these trees. Be mindful of required setbacks from wetlands, too. Many townships won't even allow you to drive a single fence post within a certain distance of deemed wetlands without applying for a variance. You can often get into big trouble if you try to ignore the powers that be.

PREVAILING WINDS. If you live in a rather windy area, you should design your tree house appropriately, or not build in that location at all. Figure out what direction the wind most often originates from and consider making your structure a bit more aerodynamic, or at least not positioning the largest face of your tree house so that it receives all of this wind. An open decklike tree house (no walls) might be a better fit for such an area, letting the wind pass right through the structure.

> SOLAR GAIN. I've built many clear-sided tree houses that receive comments such as, "You're going to roast alive in there!" or "In the summer this place will be a coffin!" What these people fail to realize is that I've already taken solar gain and solar orientation into consideration. I usually position my builds under deciduous trees, so that in the summer they are shaded and remain cool, even with greenhouse-like walls. Conversely, in the winter, when the leaves drop, the sun serves as a free heat source by passive solar gain, and you'll need less by way of heating for your space in the daytime.

SURROUNDING TREES. Are there any massive and ill trees nearby that might threaten your build down the road? If so, consider a site elsewhere, or it might be time to transform those old and unstable widow-makers into firewood. Removing large trees can be a time-consuming, expensive, and even dangerous job, so take that into consideration, too. Do you really want this one specific site, or are there options elsewhere before you whip out your wallet?

> THE VIEW. This one might seem like common sense, but I can't tell you how many tree houses, or homes, I have seen that absolutely blow this one. Take time to plan the orientation of your tree house so that its largest windows and/or its outdoor deck (if it has one) face the very best views your land has to offer. Also take time in determining the approach to your tree house. How will people arrive at it and what do you want them to see first? First impressions are everything. The approach end doesn't always have to be the entrance, either. This is very important with tree houses that are built for rentals, as this first vantage is the photo that will most often be taken by guests (and shared).

NEIGHBORS. If they're going to be able to see the tree house at all, make sure you clear the project with them. They'll appreciate it and often won't have any issues with your tree house endeavors; they might even be excited about the whole ordeal. My tree house office at home lies about 12 feet from my neighbor's property line, and I was certain to talk to them before attaching even a single board to a tree. I also buttered them up by mentioning that they could use or enjoy the tree house anytime they wanted and could even allow their traveling friends to crash in it should they want to. Being open with your neighbors goes a long way.

ACCESS. While remoteness and privacy can be a great thing, keep access in mind. You're going to be lugging *lots* of materials out to your building site. If you have to cross three streams and a rope bridge or two to get your supplies to the site, you'll be less likely to finish the darn thing. I contradict my own advice with the Renegade Tree House (page 17), but I did intentionally keep that build incredibly small because of the long lumber-trekking that I knew would be in store. During my run as an HGTV host, we did one remote build because the producers thought the strife of getting material deep into the woods would make for great TV. It was a total pain and ate up so much of our limited build time that they soon regretted it.

PRIVACY. If you plan on building a tree house for guests to stay in, you might not want it looming a few feet away from your own bedroom window. Even more so, you wouldn't want it intruding on those living near you. For year-round seclusion, pick a site that is obscured by evergreens. If you choose to go the renegade approach and build without permission, you should heed this advice. Tree houses that are not within eyesight of the road or any public area are less likely to have problems because few people will even know they exist. Most tree house teardown stories originate with neighbors that feel their view has been spoiled by a build, so perhaps plant your structure, if possible, where no one is likely to see it at all. As we mentioned earlier, "Out of sight, out of mind."

⋀ SLOPE. While it could be advantageous to build a tree house on steep land that otherwise might not be fit for normal dwellings, do remember that doing all your cutting and framing work on unlevel sites is very awkward. Steep slopes aid in cheating the height of a tree house by the nature of the structure rising away from the drop of the land, but they can be extremely tough worksites. I recommend that you consider building an initial lower "ground" deck first so that you have a flat, clean, and level workspace if you aren't going to be prefabricating your wall pieces off-site.

TEN TOOLS TO TAKE TO THE TREE HOUSE

MANY PARTICIPANTS OF MY HANDS-ON WORKSHOPS have asked me, "Deek, what bare-minimum tools would I need to build a simple tree house or tiny cabin?" The answer isn't universally applicable, but here are the tools I think you would need to tackle most builds. Yes, you could work with less, and I have. In fact, I've done a few backwoods builds with zero power tools in tow (all hammer-and-nails work and handsaw cuts), but for the sake of time, your patience, your back, and your mental well-being, it might be smart to invest in a few of the following.

NOTE: I've omitted the more obvious and simple items, such as pencils, ear protection, tape measures (though you should get a good, wide 25-foot-long one), and work gloves. Most people picking up this book likely have those already. If you don't, get shopping!

1. **IMPACT DRIVER.** This might be the most important tool. Buy a good one, as you will often need to drive some rather huge lag screws or TimberLOK screws and make some large holes (for the installation of TABs). Since you might be doing a lot of climbing and ladder work, do not buy the corded version. You'll want something high-powered and lightweight. The alternative to using an impact driver is to hand-screw things, which will be punishing on your hands and wrists and gets old really fast. I am very happy with my Milwaukee impact driver with lithium-ion batteries. There are plenty of other great makes and models out there, though.

2. **HANDSAW.** I am partial to the Stanley FATMAX line, which is affordable enough. You can even get short handsaws that will fit inside most toolboxes.

3. **16-OUNCE HAMMER.** Yes, I own a framing hammer, but I don't feel it's needed to drive even the largest of nails. A 16-ounce one seems to be a good middle-of-the-road choice for most people and most builds. People a bit daintier in frame could go with a 12-ounce hammer, but the lighter tool will require three times the "whacks" to drive most fasteners.

4. **MITER SAW.** Also referred to as a chop saw or drop saw, this is the most expensive item on this list, but it's incredibly valuable when it comes to clean and precise cuts of any angle. A sliding compound miter saw (the saw blade slides back and forth to enable it to cut wider planks) is a good idea for long-term use and complex projects. However, they usually are not very portable. A decent battery-operated chop saw, though pricey, is good for an off-grid build—just be sure to bring lots of charged batteries.

5. **SPEED SQUARE.** These li'l suckers have about a hundred uses, and if you get a metal one, you will never have to buy a replacement. Great for old-school handsaw cuts in the field, for figuring out angles, and for stabilization or as a guide rail for your circular saw cuts, they can even open a bottle of beer. They are often dull gray in color, so I always blast mine with a little neon spray paint so that it visually stands out.

6. **BATTERY-OPERATED CIRCULAR SAW.** Everyone has their favorites. My go-to is Milwaukee. The battery life and power keep getting better and better on these as technology progresses. A circular saw will reduce your saw work by 400 percent, and to me that is money well spent when time is of the essence.

7. **4-FOOT LEVEL.** This is a must for getting true levels and making sure any posts or walls are plumb (vertically straight). Don't get a flimsy tin one; it should be structurally stout enough that you don't have to ever worry about it getting bent. Levels that aren't as long will not give you as accurate a reading.

8. **PRY BAR/CROWBAR.** You will mess up, or you will need to disassemble something, lever something heavy into place, or adjust a wall or board by force at some point. I promise you it will happen. Furthermore, if you plan on salvaging materials or employing any forklift pallet wood into any project of yours, this is a good tool to have on your side.

9. **TOOL BELT OR NAIL POUCH.** These save you from having to climb up and down ladders to get things. They can hold a good variety of screws, bits, your tape measure, ear protection, your cell phone (in case you need help or fall), and whatever else, all within your immediate grasp.

10. **NAIL PULLER.** Basically a pocket-size crowbar for digging under nailheads to pull them out, this is great to have if you plan on salvaging a lot of materials for your build.

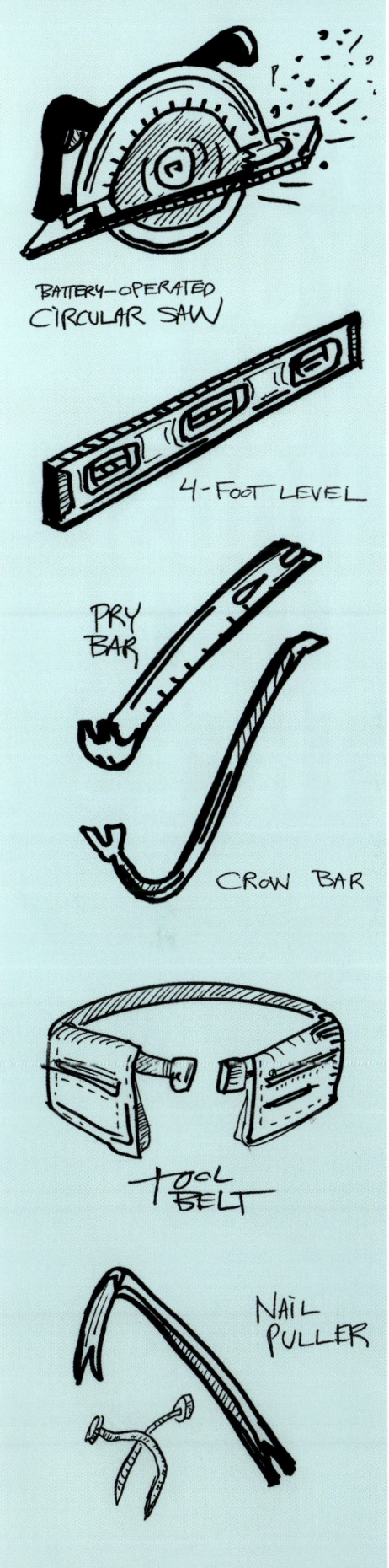

BATTERY-OPERATED CIRCULAR SAW

4-FOOT LEVEL

PRY BAR

CROW BAR

TOOL BELT

NAIL PULLER

AFFIXING YOUR TREE HOUSE TO THE TREES

When working single-handedly, I screw a 2×10 girder in place temporarily until I can get it perfectly level by walking to each end and adjusting as necessary.

TREE HOUSE TABS (tree house attachment bolts) are one of the most important hardware elements in any tree house build. They consist of a thick steel disc, through which goes a long, threaded steel rod that is screwed into the tree. They act as engineered "tree limbs" on which the supports of a tree house can perch, rest, or hang.

Extremely strong, TABs have quickly become the standard in the world of tree building. As a tree grows, it expands, growing outward and around the TAB, so the tree isn't harmed or stressed. As the tree grows, the TAB actually becomes even more seated within the mass of the tree. The unobtrusive shaft and shape of the TAB is also designed to prevent the tree from pushing away the tree house's supporting beams as it grows. Another huge benefit of TABs is that they are specifically designed to allow for the tree's movement, thus reducing the chance of anything failing or being pulled apart due to a windstorm or normal tree swaying over time.

While TABs work very well for both the tree house and the tree, they do have one drawback: price. Engineered TABs and Garnier Limbs (another name for attachment brackets specifically designed for tree houses by Michael Garnier) can be costly—especially if you need a few of

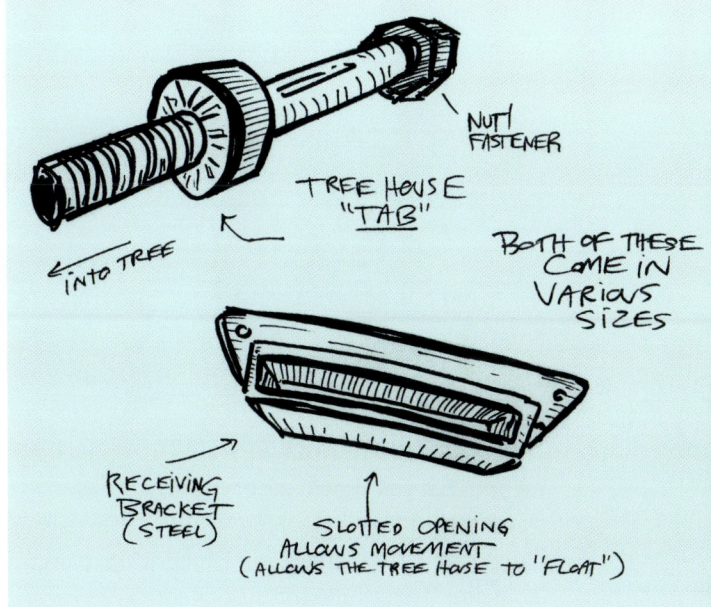

them. Often priced at $200 apiece (or far more, depending on the variety) and requiring additional fittings and accessories, TABs can quickly swell expenses. You might be dropping $1,000 before you buy one single plank of lumber.

While I prefer TABs, they just might not be feasible for builders on a budget. So are there alternatives to TABs in these cases? While this is an unpopular opinion to some, I believe that you don't absolutely need TABs to build a sound tree house that won't damage the tree on which it rests. If you are building a small tree house on a budget, you could go the old-school route and use lag screws. The key word is *small*: I wouldn't recommend lag screws for large builds. Just make sure you take into account the following considerations.

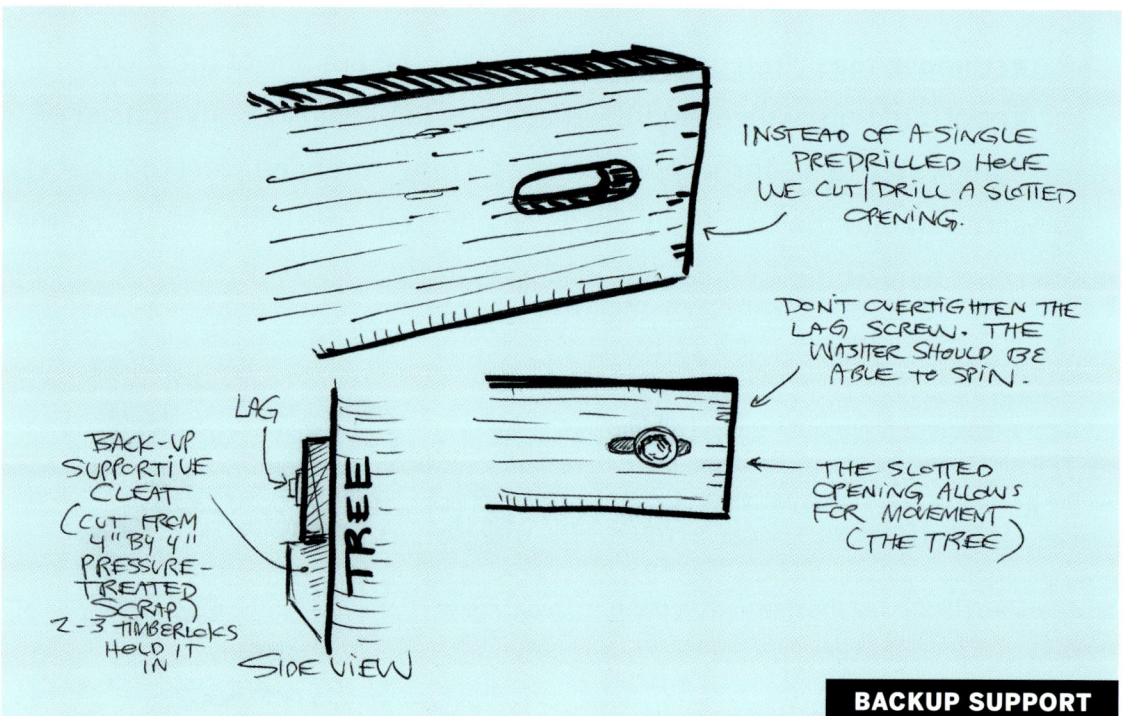

INSTEAD OF A SINGLE PREDRILLED HOLE WE CUT/DRILL A SLOTTED OPENING.

DON'T OVERTIGHTEN THE LAG SCREW. THE WASHER SHOULD BE ABLE TO SPIN.

BACK-UP SUPPORTIVE CLEAT (CUT FROM 4" BY 4" PRESSURE-TREATED SCRAP) 2-3 TIMBERLOKS HOLD IT IN

LAG

TREE

SIDE VIEW

THE SLOTTED OPENING ALLOWS FOR MOVEMENT (THE TREE)

BACKUP SUPPORT

TREES ARE INCREDIBLY RESILIENT. People may tell you that you should never use lag screws in a tree because they will kill the tree. Well, I've used old-fashioned lag screws and TimberLOKs (very large and strong industrial hex-head screws) and have yet to have a problem with any trees getting sick or dying, nor have I had any difficulties with the tree house supports or the structure itself. One major reason for this is because I only select large and healthy trees of certain species to support my builds. I also monitor those structures a bit more frequently than the tree houses made with TABs, to determine if any necessary adjustments might be needed. If monitoring your build sounds like a hassle to you and isn't going to be realistic, go the TAB route.

TREES MOVE A LOT. So your means of attachment must allow for this movement. When using lag screws, leave a little float room by doing two things: Don't ratchet the lag too tightly against the tree (making sure the washer behind the lag head is able to spin freely), and add an elongated precut hole in the support girder for the large lag, to allow for a little shifting. This method works best when attaching to lower heights on stout trees, as these trees are less likely to move so much, if at all.

TREES WIDEN AS THEY GROW. Your attachment point will not rise in height as much as it will instead slowly receive pressure from the tree's expanding diameter. Over time this could cause a few problems. For one, a board that has become too tight against a tree could promote a sunless area of future rot. Plus, with continual pressure over time, some of the lag heads—or the shafts themselves—could pop or break. It is for this reason that I recommend you work in a fail-safe, should your structure become compromised.

FAIL-SAFES IF NOT USING TABS

ADD A POST OR TWO BENEATH YOUR STRUCTURE.
This diverts some of the weight away from the tree. If positioned correctly, these posts may continue to hold the tree house up in the event of lag failure, or at least support it long enough for damage to be spotted and easily corrected.

USE THE NATURAL SUPPORTIVE V JUNCTIONS OF A TREE WHERE POSSIBLE.
Let these junctions hold parts of your tree house. Keep in mind that a moving or swaying tree house will wear at the limb through repeat abrasion. Be sure to cushion your support girder so that it won't damage the crotch of the tree. I've seen people cushion trees with pieces of old car tires, inner tube rubber, and so on. The idea is to protect the tree but still allow for movement.

ADD CRADLE CHAINS.
These can be bolted into the main supports of a tree house and attached to a higher point. I've even seen quite a few tree houses that were solely hung by support chains or cables. If the lags ever give, or shift, these heavy-duty chains will save your butt or buy you time.

ADD A SECONDARY CLEAT OR LEDGE-LIKE SUPPORT.
This will help the tree bear the weight of the structure. These supportive cleats are also lagged to the tree, so only use with very large trees that can stand the additional penetration into the tree trunk. Whenever possible, do not penetrate the tree along the same vertical line twice, as it promotes splitting and can lead to other damage and disease or infestation. The lags holding the cleats up also need to be watched over time. ▼

TIPS TO SAVE EVEN MORE MONEY

'VE ALREADY POINTED OUT WAYS in which you can save money (and time) in the tree house features, but here are a few more ways to keep items out of the landfill while infusing some coolness, originality, and interest into your tree house. We do a lot of brainstorming on ways to reuse at the Relaxshacks hands-on building workshops that I've held for more than a decade up at my Vermont camp. I often find that once people try out a few of these ideas, their creative floodgates open and give them a new mindset about "junk." I've made a good deal of my living turning roadside freebies into other things and selling them, and I have saved enormous sums of money using free supplies for my tree house builds.

FREEBIE BUNK LADDERS

It's pretty simple: Find a free bunk bed ladder or search any used markets for them. You can use the rest of the bunk bed wood for other things, too, if you have to take it all. By doing this you've just saved yourself the time and money you would have needed to fabricate one. You'd be surprised at how often wooden bunk beds are tossed. Most of their small ladders are built to hold up to 200 pounds or more, but if you're worried, just add a little hardware reinforcement (metal L brackets). And if the ladder isn't tall enough, consider building it atop a box perch—one that serves as a landing, a seat, *and* storage within or beneath it. Furthermore, some of the dismantled wood from the main bed itself can be used for interior trim, decorative accents, or built-ins. >

BED SLATS

Basic wooden bed slats are a great item to repurpose. I've harvested them a few dozen times. Clean, attractive, and strong, the wood can be used for quite a number of things, such as small shelves, desktops, and even wall cladding. However, using too much of any decorative product will eventually add a great deal of weight to a tree house, so be mindful of that.

PALLET DECONSTRUCTION METHODS – FOUR!

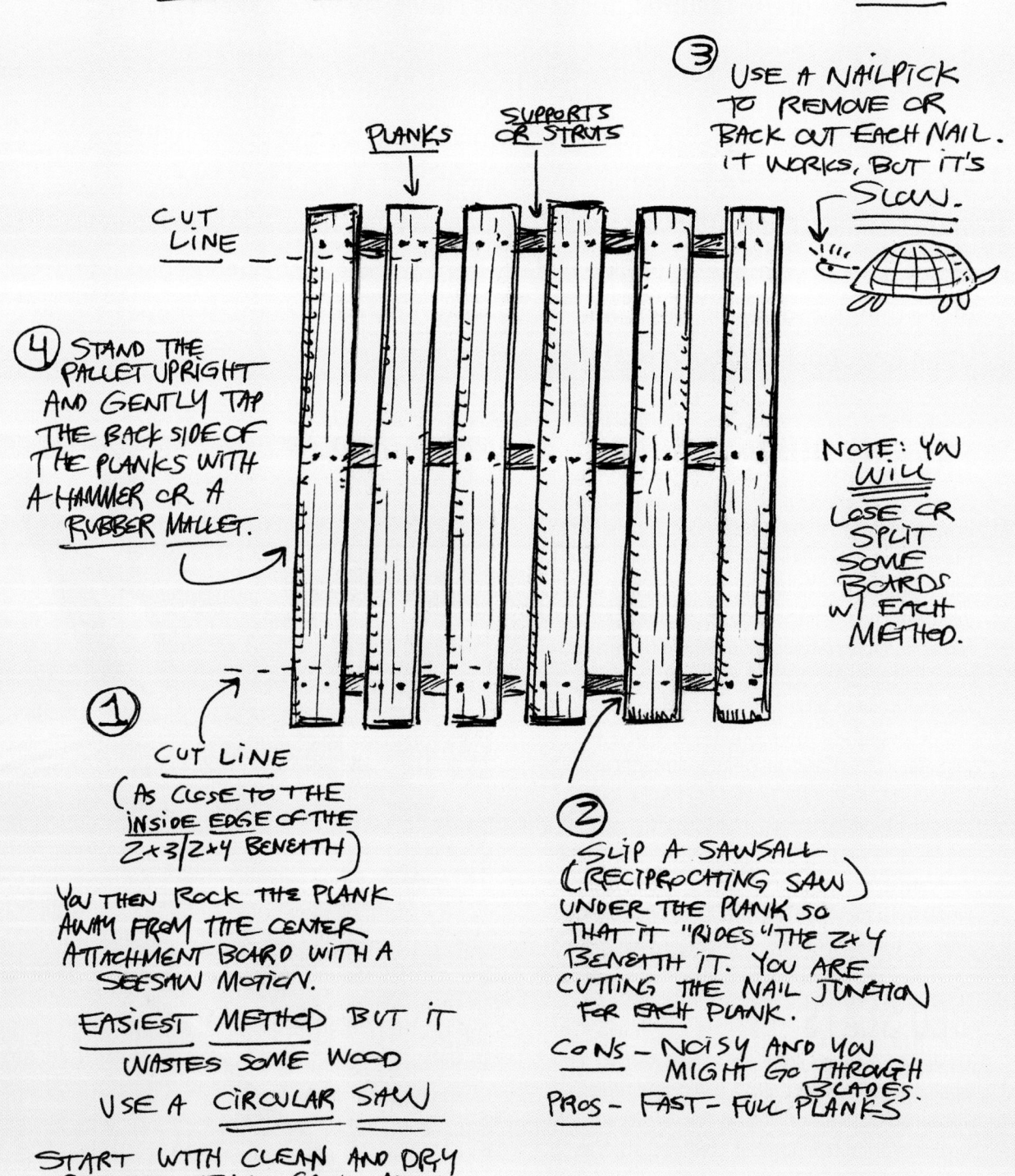

PLANKS

SUPPORTS OR STRUTS

CUT LINE

③ USE A NAILPICK TO REMOVE OR BACK OUT EACH NAIL. IT WORKS, BUT IT'S SLOW.

④ STAND THE PALLET UPRIGHT AND GENTLY TAP THE BACK SIDE OF THE PLANKS WITH A HAMMER OR A RUBBER MALLET.

NOTE: YOU WILL LOSE OR SPLIT SOME BOARDS W/ EACH METHOD.

① CUT LINE
(AS CLOSE TO THE INSIDE EDGE OF THE 2×3/2×4 BENEATH)

YOU THEN ROCK THE PLANK AWAY FROM THE CENTER ATTACHMENT BOARD WITH A SEESAW MOTION.

EASIEST METHOD BUT IT WASTES SOME WOOD

USE A CIRCULAR SAW

START WITH CLEAN AND DRY PALLETS IF YOU CAN – AVOID THE BUSTED ONES.

② SLIP A SAWSALL (RECIPROCATING SAW) UNDER THE PLANK SO THAT IT "RIDES" THE 2×4 BENEATH IT. YOU ARE CUTTING THE NAIL JUNCTION FOR EACH PLANK.

CONS – NOISY AND YOU MIGHT GO THROUGH BLADES.

PROS – FAST – FULL PLANKS

PALLET WOOD

It's free, it's everywhere, and it's the subject of 42,000 Pinterest posts that make it look so effortless. Be warned, though: Pallets are time-consuming to dismantle, and the wood is heavy and can be a mess. Pallet wood can be great for accents, shelving, and trim, but don't go overboard and use it to make much more of your build unless you're a glutton for labor. If you still don't want to listen to me, there are several ways to take these suckers apart—as shown on the opposite page.

CREATIVE CABINET PULLS

If you need pulls for doors or cabinets, consider sourcing them from natural branches. Just strip the bark and give them a quick clear finish for a little shine and to protect them. Old spoons (especially the ornate ones) also work great for these tasks. Just pilot a hole in each end, bend into the curve you desire, attach them, and voilà! You can also make simple pulls from scrap wood by cutting an oblong or half-moon shape into the backside of a small, thick board. The cut-away area gives you space for your fingers when grasping the handle. And then there's my all-time favorite: Lincoln Log toys. We used these in the documentary movie *The Box Truck Film* and people loved them. It's been our most copied idea by far.

BELT HINGES

This is an old-school "Yankee ingenuity" trick, and it works. If you need simple hinges for a small window, cabinets, or an awning-style opening, just take the leather from a well-loved and dump-bound belt and use this flexible and durable material as you would a hinge. The same can be done with canvas belts, too. It's hokey, but it does work. I've even seen people edge desks, tables, and shelves with leather belts. Chainsaw chains, when taken apart in short lengths, can also make for very industrial makeshift hinges.

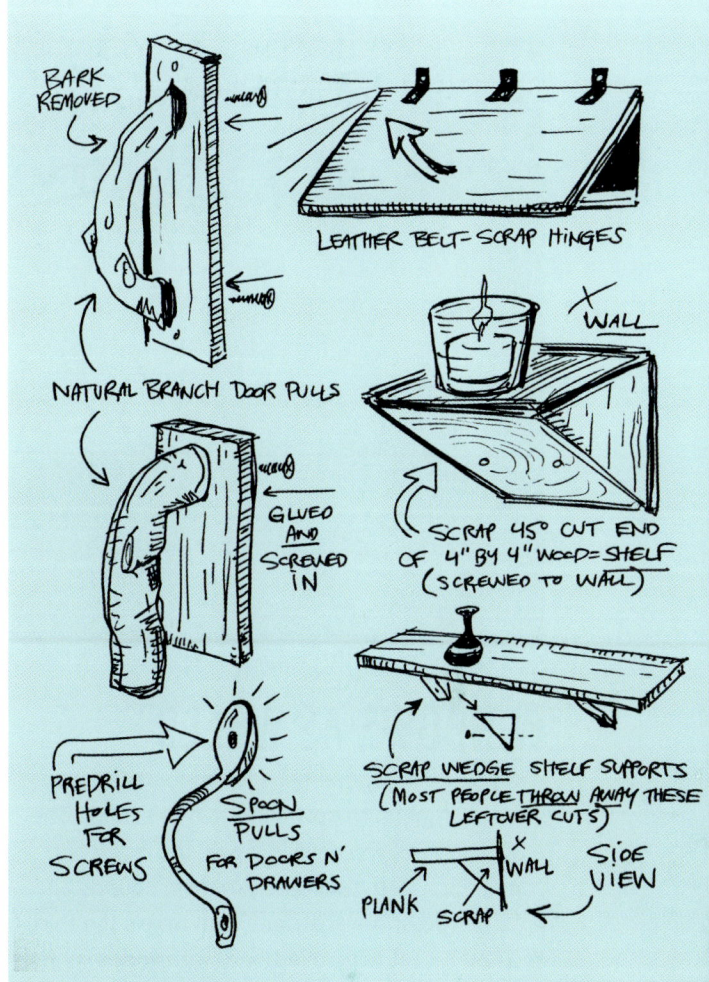

THE CRUD-PAINT SLOP-OVER

Most of you who have done any sort of building, remodeling, or home improvement have most likely collected a rather impressive array of house paints that are either never wanted again or are unusable by the time you get around to them. To combat this problem, I take inventory of my older paints and mix them into a "use it up" slurry. The result is almost always gray, and that's okay! Gray is a great color for floors inside a tree house because it can help hide tracked-in dirt. Using what you've got saves money and gets that old stuff out of the house, shed, or garage before it's fully worthless.

WINDOWS AS WALLS

Windows can frequently be found for free. I have so many that I turn down offers at this point. The more windows you have in a wall, the less wood you need to fill it, saving you money. Sounds pretty straightforward, right? But here's the thing: You don't want to go overboard with your expanse of windows. Aside from unnecessary solar gain (unless you're looking for that), windows aren't lending any structural strength. By omitting the wood usually present in a wall, your tree house will be more prone to rack (go out of square). This is not a good thing.

Glass is not a forgiving material—flex windows too far and the glass breaks. Sure, there are ways to rebuild strength in a wall through headers, bracing, and hardware, but again, you're looking for a balance between weight and strength, never mind the fact that these extras will cost you money. Again, though, windows, or even just the sashes, are often free and curbside. If you can't find them for nothing, look to your local online secondhand markets.

MILK CRATES

For those of you who went to college, milk crate bookshelves and record bins were a staple—a cheap, often ugly staple. If you gussy up those free crates, you can have some nice furnishing for your tree house. I've seen console benches for entryways fashioned from milk crates but made to look more attractive by merely giving them a slab wood top. (You can see one crate-version stool in the A-Frame Tree House on page 213.)

You can also face the opening of these crates downward, add four scrap wood legs, and create a rather sturdy seat or side table (or both). Give it a nice-looking top, perhaps cobbled together from some thin leftover scraps that you can glue together, and you're left with something far more palatable than its original form.

TAR PAPER

No money? Budget real tight? Well, you might get five years out of a tar-paper roof (held down with wood batten strips) on your no-frills kids' tree house. Worst case, you replace it a few years down the road with the remainder of the roll you never fully used up.

DRESSER DRAWERS

People junk old dressers all the time in this era of poorly built goods and furnishings with limited life spans. It's a terrible thing, really, that people would rather buy new than attempt to fix anything (or build or buy anything made to last to begin with), but at least you and I can benefit from this! If the dresser itself is a mess and not worth saving (or breaking your back to haul), often the drawers are in fine condition. Grab them! Give them casters and use as rolling storage under the bed, mount on walls as shelving, or stack and fasten together to create a spread of storage cubbies or display cubes. Or bust up the drawers and use the resulting wood for wall paneling, slabs for artwork (as you would a canvas), and even interior trim in any build. I've done all of these things, and they all work well and require almost no skill to execute.

SIMPLE PLYWOOD FLOORS

If you want to save weight, time, and money, use simple ¾-inch plywood as your flooring. It's a tree house, not a mansion. If you buy a slightly higher grade of the stuff and add a few clear coats to it, it'll actually look very nice. Some people even strive for this stark industrial or almost Danish-modern look. Just don't cheap out and buy or use anything thinner than ¾ inch, as you're apt to get what we refer to as "trampoline floors" from the way they sag and bounce.

ELECTION SIGNS

Those nonrecyclable signs that populate lawns and busy intersections during election cycles are made of something called coroplast. The stuff is darn durable and won't decay in a landfill anytime soon. I have used these for roofing a tree house in the same way that one would affix wood shingles. This works well if it's a roof so high up that no one ever has to see the election message.

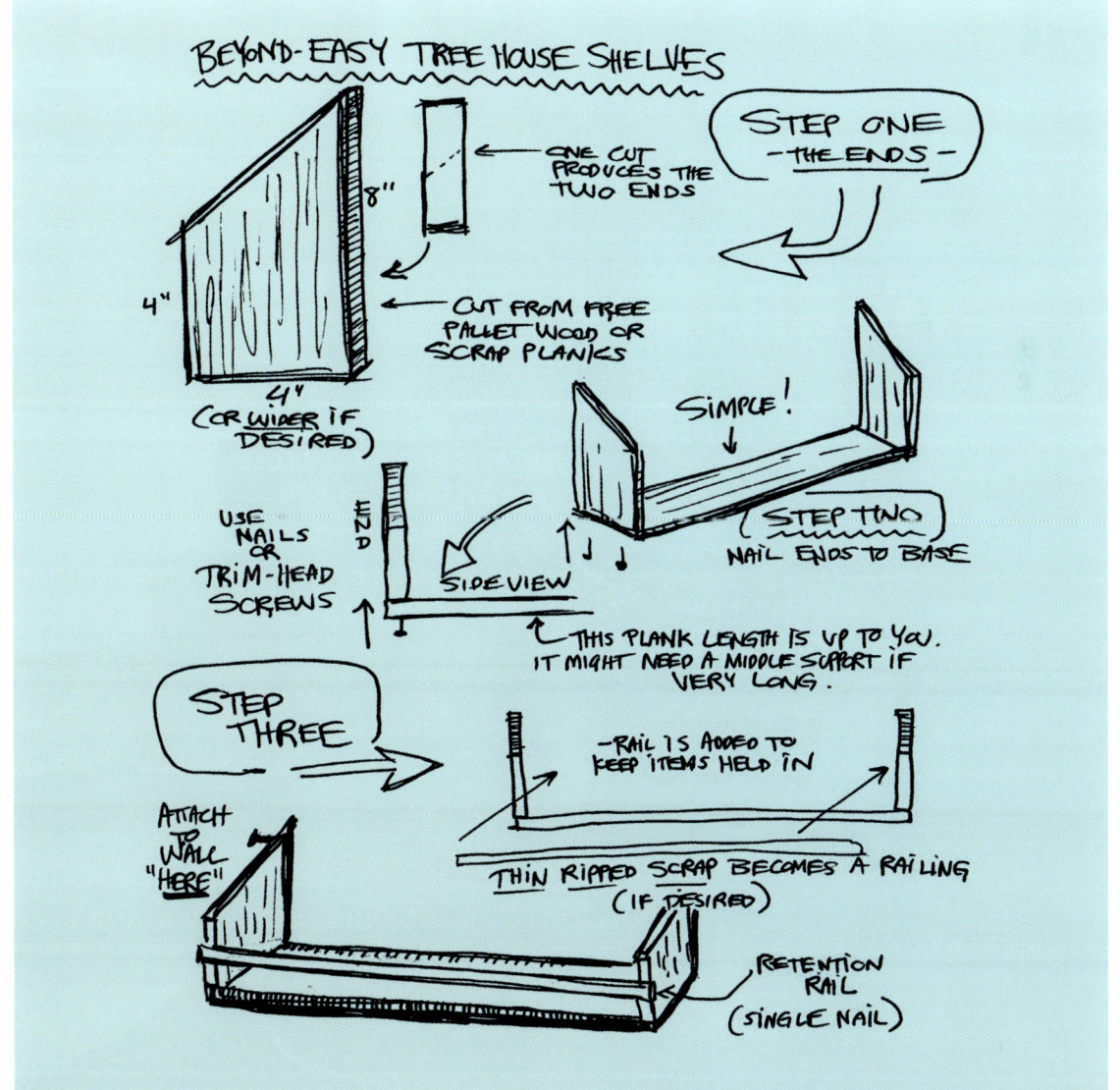

MORE REUSE!

Lessons from a Fairly Famous Home

HERE ARE SOME MORE TIPS for using reused material to save money. Not all that long ago, a film director by the name of Alex Eaves and I teamed up for a documentary film that was to chronicle the step-by-step journey of building a tiny home on wheels. The catch? Well, this home was to be constructed with almost nothing but reused, secondhand, found, and even dumpster-dived materials. Could it be done? You'll have to check out *The Box Truck Film* . . . though the photos below really give away the answer.

While we can all agree that this isn't a tree house, you could work all of these ideas into your tree house build to save a very good deal of loot. Well over 90 percent of what you see in these photos was on its way to a landfill and rescued. Remember: There are second-life possibilities for most items, and this reimagining can be not only fun but also effective and even attractive.

PART OF LADDER BECOMES A SHELF/SPICE RACK

WINDOW FLOOR MODEL

LOBSTER POT TURNED INTO A WORKING SINK

METAL DOOR THRESHOLD AS A BACKSPLASH

LINCOLN LOG CLOSET DOOR PULL

DRUMSTICK DRAWER HANDLE

DISCARDED TV STAND BECOMES KITCHEN BASE/CABINET

REUSED ITEM DOUBLES AS ART AND SHELF

SECONDHAND DOOR

FREE PALLET WOOD

SKATEBOARD TRUCK AXLE DOOR HANDLE

CHAIR FROM THE SIDE OF THE ROAD THAT WE FIXED

WALL ART OPENS UP FOR STORAGE

SCRAP PLY AND PALLET WOOD (FRAMING) BENCH

FREE DRESSER DRAWER (WE BUILT A FRAME AROUND IT)

PART 3

STEP-BY-STEP SAMPLE BUILD

HERE I HAVE CHRONICLED most of the building journey of one simple little tree house my son Jonas and I built for the child of a client. With only two and a half days to build, I knew it had to be fairly straightforward, but at the same time I wanted it to be a bit funky, fun, and unusual. I also aimed to make it rather colorful where possible, while not going overboard, so that it would also be appealing to adults. I decided to take the simple and time-saving approach of an A-frame design, but with the incorporation of lightweight knee walls (short side walls) to make it more spacious.

It is my hope that you not only learn a few things from this build but also gain some inspiration in a "Hey, that's not rocket science—I can do that!" sense.

NEW YORK A-FRAME

TRIANGULAR WINDOW FLIPS OPEN

LAG SCREW OR "TAB" TO TREE

PRESSURE-TREATED POSTS

HANG SPACE BENEATH

ATTACHED TO TREE BY "TAB" OR LAGS/CLEAT

PREBUILD

I prebuilt the walls of the tree house in the convenience of my own home near Boston (tools within reach, power available, easy access) before later hauling them out to New York. This gave me a jump start on the build, too, when I had only a finite number of days to work on the project.

SELECTING THE SITE

This spot was a cool, natural little grove that was private yet close enough to the house that it could be seen and monitored by the parents. Large enough for what we had planned, the tree had a lot of character as well.

HAMMER

SETTING THE POSTS

My son Jonas set and plumbed the posts. Each one sits on a wide granite stone in each hole to spread out its weight, preventing it from being driven downward over time.

It's best to use store-bought hardware post cradles that are set in concrete, but in a time crunch, you can set posts this way. After we backfilled the holes with concrete and stones, we held the posts in place temporarily with angle braces. We often load the end of the post with quite a few large galvanized nails to act as makeshift rebar to hold things in place. These 16-penny nailheads become imbedded in the concrete as it cures.

TIP: An old Vermonter trick is to add a few "cheater stones" when you backfill with concrete. These help wedge the post in place for leveling/plumbing while the concrete dries, and make the concrete go farther.

We sloped the concrete cap for water drainage, and once it cured, we caulked the gap between the concrete and the wood with silicone caulking.

BUILDING THE CROSS SUPPORTS

The cross supports will ultimately help us seat the fully built base when we lift it in place. Here we set and leveled one of the main cross supports.

LEVEL

Check to make sure all is level before proceeding—this is a simple and hugely important step. Make sure to recheck it before you drive any screws home. You can also see that we left the area beneath the tree house high enough so that most people could walk beneath it, or make use of the space.

IMPACT DRIVER

We put in a screw to hold the main supports in place, then stepped back to assess the work and make sure all was still level. Only then did we drive the rest of the screws or lags in. Ultimately, we'd use a very large lag or two to support most of the weight on this end of the build.

When holding and stabilizing the initial supports, don't be afraid to ask for a helping hand.

BUILDING THE BASE AND FLOOR

We built the simple base on the ground to save time and to avoid aerial work as much as possible.

With a base this small, it's not too much of a problem to transport and then lift it into place.

To make sure our walls wouldn't bind against the tree's lean, we held up a board vertically. In this case they would have, so we knew to slide the base away from the tree a few inches to gain the clearance we wanted (also accounting for sway and movement of the tree in heavy winds).

Plywood is heavy (especially ¾-inch sheets), so don't be afraid to ask for help lifting it into place if you're struggling. With Jonas on top, we were able to pull the sheet into place from above.

With the base attached, Jonas squared ¾-inch plywood sheets I passed up to him to the base's edge.

SPEED SQUARE

Make sure everything is square and still properly spaced before nailing the plywood in place.

TIP: In many cases it can be easier and quicker to cut off extra plywood after you've attached it to the base.

We nailed the plywood floor in place, then we chalked a line to cut off the extra floor.

A straight board aids in penciling cut lines for excess plywood. Be sure it's a nice straight one, though!

CIRCULAR SAW

Cutting off the excess base plywood with a circular saw

SMART LIMB REMOVAL

It's much easier to remove any remaining branches in the way while standing on the platform than while standing on a ladder.

We added these diagonal supports to give the odd base a bit of flair. They also made use of the extended horizontal support.

We secured the side bracket after a long angle cut.

I will often widen the "foot" of the tree house with some scraps. This board is attached to the post with several screws and sits on the concrete hub. If the post were to ever soften at the bottom of the hole, this would help support the tree house and buy it time.

ATTACHING TO THE TREE

TIP: If needed, the lags and screws should be backed out a half-turn or so each year as the tree widens with growth.

Angular base supports add strength and stability to the tree house.

The supports sat on some simple shelf cleats cut from 4×4 pressure-treated scraps. These cleats were attached to the tree with TimberLOK screws to serve as backup or doubled support.

The entranceway deck gives the tree a little breathing room for future growth. The supports seen at left and right are designed to move with the tree.

FUTURE
TREE
HOUSE

PREPPING THE WALLS

All of this work was done on the ground, as it's far easier to work this way as opposed to up in a tree or from a ladder.

With the base almost done, Jonas rolled two or three coats of paint onto the simple end walls that we built with 2×3s and ⅜-inch plywood. This gauge plywood is strong enough for tree house walls, but still light enough to lift up and into place.

The triangular window will lift open, so we intentionally left a good deal of overhanging Sunlite Multiwall material so that it will properly shed rain.

Two leftover angle scraps filled in the top void, which will serve as a fixed (non-opening) window for natural light. This Sunlite Multiwall was affixed with roofing screws (with neoprene washers for compression sealing).

Hinges were added, then the triangular window was attached to the front wall so that it would swing outward as an "awning window."

Adding simple trim—like these furring strip boards—to any structure spruces up its look and gives weight and clean definition to its outside edge. These boards are very inexpensive, too!

You'll notice quite a difference in look between the front (trimmed) and back wall. We'll soon trim the back wall as well.

We checked the back wall and its trim before beginning installation up on the base. You'll notice that the door opening hasn't been cut yet as we were still debating where to place it.

The ground-built pieces were carried over for assembly.

PUTTING THE WALLS IN PLACE

The back wall went up first, since it wouldn't be in the way as we lifted up the other walls.

Then we loaded the short side walls.

Things started to take shape. To me, this is the most exciting part of the build as you start to see results so quickly.

You'll notice that we left an open gap near the peak. That was for ventilation and will later be screened in.

We put the front wall securely in place.

BUILDING THE ROOF

Once the ridge board was screwed into place, we could begin adding the rafters.

We found the measurements for one rafter and then used it as a template to cut all the others.

Because we used 2×4 rafters, we didn't notch them. We fastened them from above and screwed them in from underneath the top plate of the short side wall to hold them in place.

Here we started to install the roof decking or planks. You can see the 4-foot level we used to make sure that the initial board was perfectly horizontal.

We opted not to use tar paper beneath the Suntuf roofing. The client didn't want it, preferring the striped effect the roof had without it. Also, because the slope of the roof was so steep and the Suntuf was very durable, not to mention the fact that the roof planking was all shiplap, we didn't need it. But tar paper is not a bad idea if you have the time.

Jonas was getting ready to begin work on the other side. Note: The undercarriage or space beneath the tree house is a perfect place to store lumber and other materials in case of rain, especially if your build will take several days.

Here we made use of the roof cutoffs from the other side as we began filling in the skylight side of the tree house. Use what you've got and try to plan efficiently with lumber usage.

A large plank or two threaded through and across the interior of the tree house served as makeshift staging to help reach the higher areas of the roof.

The roof was designed so that a standard 8-foot sheet of Suntuf polycarbonate would extend a bit beyond its bottom edge to effectively shed rain and protect the plywood sides.

MAKING THE DECK/LANDING

The tiny deck or landing was made separately using 2×6 lumber, then placed atop the main tree house supports and secured with long screws. It's easier to build a small deck like this on the ground where it's safer and you have more room to maneuver. If the deck were larger, we would have assembled it up in the tree.

PENCIL

A carpenter's pencil served as a spacer. This gap allows for the expansion of the lumber and for proper deck drainage.

We left the boards "whole" and snapped a line and cut off the excess when the deck was done. It saves a little bit of time and ensures a nice, clean cut line for the deck's edge.

One of the boards overhung a little bit too much, so we fixed it with a rip cut.

3,2,1...

...LiFT!

The deck was lifted into place. Note that the main large lag screw wasn't even installed yet into the tree. This is a testament to how strong just a few TimberLOK screws are. We used them until our large 1-inch lags arrived on site (they were hard to find locally, so be sure to order any "specialty" item far ahead).

Here's a view of the roofing (before installing the clear Sunlite Multiwall skylight), the cutout for the rear door, and the mini deck in place.

ADDING THE RIDGE CAP

With the roofing done and skylight (clear Sunlite Multiwall panels) about to be installed, we gave the tree house a ridge cap (to keep rain out and allow for upward ventilation) by ripping a piece of Suntuf to the size we needed. The stuff is flexible, so it worked perfectly!

ADDING THE SKYLIGHT

After precutting this sheet of Sunlite Multiwall to size with a circular saw, we slipped it into its spot, while making sure that the existing roofing overlapped it so as to keep out rain.

BUILDING AND FRAMING THE DOOR

We were sure to use up all the small scraps we had left when building and framing the door.

Jonas made trim and angled cuts for the doorway framing.

The door is attached to the tree house by its trim work. It's unconventional but simple—and it works.

The client's son, Augie, helped us test out the door.

FINISHING TOUCHES

We kept the ladder very simple.

Position the ladder at an angle that is comfortable to climb.

A few simple and low-maintenance décor pieces add some color to the space.

Angie (my daughter) finishes up some of the interior decorating.

A simple wood "kickstand" is stored within the tree house and used to prop open the front window.

RESOURCES

BIJL BOOMHUTTEN
www.bijlboomhutten.nl

FIREFLY FORTS
www.fireflyforts.com

O2 TREEHOUSE
www.o2treehouse.com

RELAX SHACKS
https://relaxshacks.blogspot.com

STILES DESIGNS
https://stilesdesigns.com

TREES & PEOPLE
www.treesandpeople.com/en

TREE TOP BUILDERS
https://treetopbuilders.net

TREEHOUSE EXPERTS
www.treehouseexperts.com

THE TREEHOUSE GUYS, LLC
https://thetreehouseguys.com

ADDITIONAL PHOTOGRAPHY CREDITS

Ali Kol, 130–133; Courtesy of Amanda McMasters, 26, 27; B'fer Roth/The Treehouse Guys, LLC, 10, 76–79; Bijl Boomhutten, 110–113, 138–142; Breathe Easy Treehouses, 91, 92, 157 r.; Carsten Ginsburg, 13, 36–39; © Chris Daniele/dirtandglass.net, 21, 32, 109; Courtesy of Derek Diedricksen, 11; Dylan Jon Wade Cox, 180, 181; Emily Gaswick, 60–65; Courtesy of Fen Druadìn, 72; Flemming Rasmussen, 2, 84–86, 87 b.; Josh Howell Photography, 5, 87 t., 88–90; Klint Kuykendall Coppertop Carpentry, 80–83; Michele Ghisletti, 3 m., 98–102; Noémie Trusty, 54, 55; O2 Treehouse, 114, 115; Rick's Services and Goods, 73–75, 161; The Treehouse Guys, LLC, 3 b., 120–125, 163 b.; Tree Top Builders staff, 134–137, 148, 149, 160; Treehouse Experts, 126–129, 171; Trees & People, IBC, 116–119; Victoria Cantwell, 6, 143–147

INDEX